200 Light
chicken dishes

200 Light
chicken dishes

hamlyn **all color**

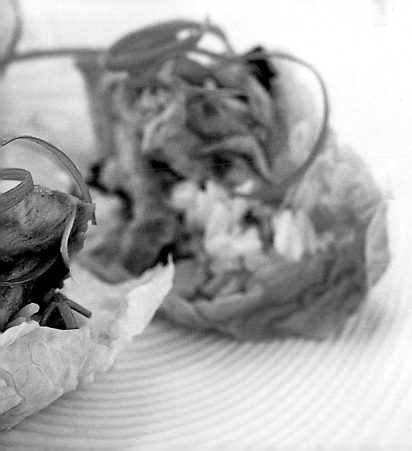

An Hachette UK Company
www.hachette.co.uk

First published in Great Britain in 2015 by Hamlyn
a division of Octopus Publishing Group Ltd
Endeavour House, 189 Shaftesbury Avenue
London, WC2H 8JY
www.octopusbooks.co.uk
www.octopusbooksusa.com

Distributed in the US by Hachette Book Group
1290 Avenue of the Americas, 4th and 5th Floors
New York, NY 10020

Distributed in Canada by Canadian Manda Group
664 Annette St, Toronto, Ontario, Canada M6S 2C8

ISBN: 978-0-600-62970-2

A CIP catalogue record for this book is available rom the
British Library.

Printed and bound in China

10 9 8 7 6 5 4 3 2 1

Standard level kitchen cup and spoon measurements are
used in all recipes

Ovens should be preheated to the specified temperature;
if using a convection oven, follow the manufacturer's
instructions for adjusting the time and temperature.

Fresh herbs, large eggs, and freshly ground black pepper
should be used unless otherwise stated.

This book includes dishes made with nuts and nut
derivatives. It is advisable for people with known allergic
reactions to nuts and nut derivatives or those who may be
potentially vulnerable to these allergies, such as pregnant
and nursing mothers, people with a weakened immune sys-
tem, the elderly, babies, and children, to avoid dishes made
with these. It is prudent to check the labels of all prepared
ingredients for the possible inclusion of nut derivatives.

contents

introduction	6
under 200 calories	18
under 300 calories	36
under 400 calories	92
under 500 calories	166
index	236
acknowledgments	240

introduction

introduction

this series

The Hamlyn All Color Light Series is a collection of handy-size books, each packed with over 200 healthy recipes on a variety of topics and cuisines to suit your needs.

The books are designed to help those people who are trying to lose weight by offering a range of delicious recipes that are low in calories but still high in flavor. The recipes show a calorie count per portion, so you will know exactly what you are eating. These are recipes for real and delicious food, not ultra-slimming meals, so they will help you maintain your new healthier eating plan for life. They must be used as part of a balanced diet, with the cakes and sweet dishes eaten only as an occasional treat.

how to use this book

All the recipes in this book are clearly marked with the number of calories (kcal) per serving. The chapters cover different calorie bands: under 500 calories, under 400 calories, etc.

There are variations on each recipe at the bottom of the page—note the calorie count as they do vary and can sometimes be more than the original recipe.

The figures assume that you are using low-fat versions of dairy products, so be sure to use skim milk and low-fat yogurt. They have also been calculated using lean meat, so make sure you trim meat of all visible fat and remove the skin from chicken breasts. Use moderate amounts of oil and butter for cooking and low-fat/low-calorie alternatives when you can.

Don't forget to take note of the number of portions each recipe makes and divide up the quantity of food accordingly, so that you know just how many calories you are consuming.

Be careful too, about side dishes and accompaniments that will also add to calorie content.

Above all, enjoy trying the new flavors and exciting recipes that this book contains. Rather than dwelling on the thought that you are denying yourself your usual unhealthy treats, think of your new regime as a positive step toward a new you. Not only will you lose weight and feel more confident, but your

health will benefit, the condition of your hair and nails will improve, and you will exude a healthy glow.

the risks of obesity

Up to half of women and two-thirds of men are overweight or obese in the developed world today. Being overweight can not only make us unhappy with our appearance, but can also lead to serious health problems, including heart disease, high blood pressure, and diabetes.

When someone is obese, it means they are overweight to the point that it could start to seriously threaten their health. In fact, obesity ranks a close second to smoking as a possible cause of cancer. Obese women are more likely to have complications during and after pregnancy, and people who are overweight or obese are also more likely to have coronary heart disease, gallstones, osteoarthritis, high blood pressure, and type 2 diabetes.

how can I tell if I am overweight?

The best way to tell if you are overweight is to work out your body mass index (BMI). If using metric measurements, divide your weight in kilograms (kg) by your height in meters (m) squared. (For example, if you are 1.7 m tall and weigh 70 kg, the calculation would be 70 ÷ 2.89 = 24.2.) If using imperial measurements, divide your weight in pounds (lb) by your height in inches (in) squared and multiply by 703.

Then compare the figure to the list below (these figures apply to healthy adults only).

Less than 20	underweight
20–25	healthy
25–30	overweight
Over 30	obese

As we all know by now, one of the major causes of obesity is eating too many calories.

what is a calorie?

Our bodies need energy to stay alive, grow, keep warm, and be active. We get the energy we need to survive from the food and drinks we consume—more specifically, from the fat, carbohydrate, protein, and alcohol that they contain.

A calorie (cal), as anyone who has ever been on a diet will know, is the unit used to measure how much energy different foods contain. A calorie can be scientifically defined as the energy required to raise the temperature of 1 gram of water from 14.5°C to 15.5°C (58.1°F to 59.9°F). A kilocalorie (kcal) is 1,000 calories and it is, in fact, kilocalories that we usually mean when we talk about the calories in different foods.

Different food types contain different numbers of calories. For example, a gram of carbohydrate (starch or sugar) provides 3.75 kcal, protein provides 4 kcal per gram, fat provides 9 kcal per gram and alcohol provides 7 kcal per gram. So, fat is the most concentrated source of energy—weight for weight, it provides just over twice as many calories as either protein or carbohydrate —with alcohol not far behind. The energy content of a food or drink depends on how many grams of carbohydrate, fat, protein, and alcohol are present.

how many calories do we need?

The number of calories we need to consume varies from person to person, but your body weight is a clear indication of whether you are eating the right amount. Body weight is simply determined by the number of calories you are eating compared to the number of calories your body is using to maintain itself and needs for physical activity. If you regularly consume more calories than you use up, you will start to gain weight as extra energy is stored in the body as fat.

Based on our relatively inactive modern-day lifestyles, most nutritionists recommend that women should aim to consume around 2,000 calories (kcal) per day, and men an amount of around 2,500. Of course, the amount of energy required depends on your level of activity: the more active you are, the more energy you need to maintain a stable weight.

a healthier lifestyle

To maintain a healthy body weight, we need to expend as much energy as we consume; to lose weight, energy expenditure must therefore exceed intake of calories. So, exercise is a vital tool in the fight to lose weight. Physical activity doesn't just help us control body weight; it also helps to reduce our appetites and is known to have beneficial effects on the heart and blood that help prevent cardiovascular disease.

Many of us claim we don't enjoy exercise and simply don't have the time to fit it into our hectic schedules. So the easiest way to increase physical activity is by incorporating it into our daily routines, perhaps by walking or cycling instead of driving (particularly for short journeys), taking up more active hobbies such as gardening, and taking small and simple steps, such as using the stairs instead of the elevator whenever possible.

As a general guide, adults should aim to do at least 30 minutes of moderate-intensity exercise, such as a brisk walk, five times a week. In place of 30 minutes three sessions of 10 minutes are just as beneficial. Children and young people should be encouraged to take at least 60 minutes of moderate-intensity exercise every day.

Some activities will use up more energy than others. The following list shows some examples of the energy a person weighing 132 lb would expend doing the following activities for 30 minutes:

activity	energy
Ironing	69 kcal
Cleaning	75 kcal
Walking	99 kcal
Golf	129 kcal
Fast walking	150 kcal
Cycling	180 kcal
Aerobics	195 kcal
Swimming	195 kcal
Running	300 kcal
Sprinting	405 kcal

body weight. Regular exercise will also make a huge difference: the more you can burn, the less you will need to diet.

improve your diet

For most of us, simply adopting a more balanced diet will reduce our calorie intake and lead to weight loss. Follow these simple recommendations:

Eat more starchy foods, such as bread, potatoes, rice, and pasta. Assuming these replace the fattier foods you usually eat, and you don't smother them with oil or butter, this will help reduce the amount of fat and increase the amount of fiber in your diet. As a bonus, try to use wholegrain rice, pasta, and flour, as the energy from these foods is released more slowly in the body, making you feel fuller for longer.

Eat more fruit and vegetables, aiming for at least five portions of different fruit and vegetables a day (excluding potatoes).

As long as you don't add extra fat to your fruit and vegetables in the form of cream, butter, or oil, these changes will help reduce your fat intake and increase the amount of fiber and vitamins you consume.

who said vegetables must be dull?

Eat fewer sugary foods, such as cookies, cakes, and candy bars. This will also help reduce your fat intake. If you fancy something sweet, aim for fresh or dried fruit instead.

make changes for life

The best way to lose weight is to try to adopt healthier eating habits that you can easily maintain all the time, not just when you are trying to slim down. Aim to lose no more than 2 lb per week to ensure you lose only your fat stores. People who go on crash diets lose lean muscle as well as fat and are much more likely to put the weight back on again soon afterward.

For a woman, the aim is to reduce her daily calorie intake to around 1,500 kcal while she is trying to lose weight, then settle on around 2,000 per day thereafter to maintain her new

Reduce the amount of fat in your diet, so you consume fewer calories. Choosing low-fat versions of dairy products, such as skim milk and low-fat yogurt, doesn't necessarily mean your food will be tasteless. Low-fat versions are available for most dairy products, including milk, cheese, yogurt, and even cream and butter.

Choose lean cuts of meat, such as Canadian bacon instead of regular bacon, and chicken breasts instead of thighs. Trim all visible fat off meat before cooking and avoid frying foods—grill or roast instead. Fish is also naturally low in fat and can make a variety of tempting dishes.

simple steps to reduce your calorie intake

Few of us have an iron will, so when you are trying to cut down make it easier on yourself by following these steps:

- Serve small portions to start with. You may feel satisfied when you have finished, but if you are still hungry you can always go back for more.
- Once you have served up your meal, put away any leftover food before you eat. Don't put heaped serving dishes on the table as you will undoubtedly pick, even if you feel satisfied with what you have already eaten.
- Eat slowly and savor your food; then you are more likely to feel full when you have finished. If you rush a meal, you may still feel hungry afterward.

- Make an effort with your meals. Just because you are cutting down doesn't mean your meals have to be low on taste as well as calories. You will feel more satisfied with a meal you have really enjoyed and will be less likely to look for comfort in a bag of chips or a bar of chocolate.
- Plan your meals in advance to make sure you have all the ingredients you need. Casting around in the pantry when you are hungry is unlikely to result in a healthy, balanced meal.
- Keep healthy and interesting snacks on hand for those moments when you need something to pep you up. You don't need to succumb to a candy bar if there are other tempting treats on offer.

chicken

Chicken is highly versatile, and with 200 recipes to choose from in this book we hope that you will be able to add some new favorites to your family's repertoire.

Much has been made in the media about the welfare of chickens during rearing. For those on a tight budget, battery-farmed chickens may be the only option. Try to use up the leftovers the following day, or use the redundant carcass to make stock, so that a more expensive free-range chicken, even if not organic, is more cost-effective. While organic, free-range chickens may not be for everyone, try to choose whole chickens and chicken joints with labels indicating that the birds have been reared humanely (for more information, consult the RSPCA in the UK or the HSUS in the USA).

hygiene essentials
• Keep raw and cooked chicken separate in the refrigerator so that raw chicken juices cannot drip onto other foods.
• Cover food dishes so that chicken does not dry out.
• Use separate boards and knives for preparing raw and cooked chicken, as well as for preparing meat and vegetables.
• Defrost frozen chicken in the refrigerator, transferring to room temperature for 1–2 hours before cooking.
• Only reheat cooked food once, and make

sure it is piping hot all the way through (don't just warm foods, especially if using the microwave).
• Raw chicken that has been defrosted can only be put back in the freezer if it has been cooked and cooled. If taken out of the freezer in a cooked state, it cannot be refrozen.
• Add a small frozen ice pack to lunchboxes, and use an insulated lunchbag so that any cooked chicken stays cold.

how to make chicken stock
Why bother making your own stock? In an age when we are all being advised to cut down on our salt consumption, homemade stock

can be salt-free; it also fits in with our general tendency to recycle all we can. If you haven't got time to make stock now, don't throw the chicken carcass out—just pack it into a plastic bag and freeze it until you do have time. The following recipe makes 5¾ cups.

chicken carcass from a roast or poached
    whole bird
2 quarts **cold water**
1 large **onion**, cut into quarters but still with
    the inner brown layer of skin attached
2 **carrots**, thickly sliced
2 **celery sticks**, thickly sliced
small bunch of **mixed fresh herbs** or a **dried**
    bouquet garni
black peppercorns

Put the chicken carcass into a large saucepan with the measured water, and add the onion, carrots, and celery. Flavor with the fresh herbs or bouquet garni and a few black peppercorns, then bring to a boil. Partially cover the top of the pan with a lid, then let simmer gently for 2 hours. Strain into a pitcher and let cool. Store in the refrigerator for 2–3 days or freeze in handy-size plastic containers or well-sealed plastic bags if the carcass had not already been frozen.

preparation
Before use, always rinse chicken well in cold water, drain well, and pat dry with paper

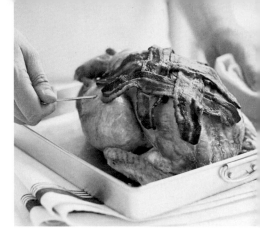

towels; this is especially important if you are using prepacked raw chicken. When rinsing a whole chicken, take extra care to rinse inside the bird, and remove giblets if included.

If using frozen chicken, make sure it is completely defrosted before use. Don't try to speed up defrosting by plunging it into warm water. Immerse in cold water and change the water frequently, or defrost in the microwave, following the manufacturer's guidelines.

is the chicken cooked?
Chicken must never be served rare or medium, but always well done. Insert a small knife into the thickest part of a joint, or through a thigh to the breast if cooking a whole chicken. The juices will run clear when the chicken is ready—if you see any traces of pink in the juices, continue cooking. If pan-frying or grilling, check at 5-minute intervals. For a whole chicken, retest after 15 minutes more in the oven.

how to joint a whole chicken

This is not as tricky as it may first seem; the secret is a good sharp knife and to locate the joints by feel before cutting through them to separate. This technique can be adapted to cut up other poultry too.

1 First remove the trussing strings and put the chicken breast side uppermost on a chopping board. Pull one leg gently away from the body. Cut through the skin between the body and leg, cut down through the meat, and then work down to the thigh joint. Bend the leg so that it eases the leg bone from its socket, then cut through the ball-and-socket joint. Repeat with the other leg.

2 To remove the wings, press one wing against the body of the bird so that both parts of the shoulder are visible. Cut through the skin, then down through the joint to sever. Tuck the wingtip under the shoulder to make a triangular-shape joint. Repeat with the other wing.

3 Split the carcass by cutting around and under both breasts with poultry shears or strong kitchen scissors. Cut through the rib cage, so separating the backbone from the breasts. Repeat on the other side.

4 Cut along the center of the breast with poultry shears, strong kitchen scissors, or a sharp knife, then either slide a knife under the breast meat on each side of the bone to release two boneless breast joints or cut straight down between the breast bone with a large cook's knife to give two joints on the bone. For a "supreme" leave the wing joint attached at step 2, but sever at the first joint so separating wing tips from body.

5 Now separate the leg joint into a drumstick and thigh. Put the joint skin side uppermost, then flex the drumstick slightly so that you can see where the central joint is. Cut through the ball-and-socket joint. Repeat with the other leg.

6 You should now have 2 drumsticks, 2 thigh joints, 2 wings, and 2 breast joints, plus a carcass (not pictured) to make stock with. When the bird is small, leave the drumstick and thigh joint joined together.

how to spatchcock a chicken or poussin (squab chicken)

Here the bird is split and then flattened so that it cooks more quickly. This enables a whole bird to be grilled, broiled, or roasted traditionally in a shorter time.

1 Put the chicken or poussin breast side

down on a chopping board and remove the trussing string. Cut the bird in half, while keeping the two halves still attached, using poultry shears or sturdy kitchen scissors.

2 Turn the bird over, then using the palm of your hand press down on the breast and flatten it slightly.

3 Trim off the knuckle bones from the drumsticks and tuck the wingtips under the bird. Neaten off any untidy skin and insert two long metal or wooden skewers through each leg, breast, and wing so that they cross under the bird and keep it flat during roasting or grilling.

how to carve a roast chicken

A good carving knife and fork are essential. Choose a knife that has a long, slightly flexible blade and a fork with tines that are close together. Even more importantly, you must keep the knife sharp. If you find using a knife steel too daunting, there are many hand or electrical knife sharpeners available from good cookshops or major department stores—it really is worth investing in one. Carve off just the amounts you need at a time, working first on one side and then on the other side of the bird, as needed. If the bird is stuffed, don't forget to serve the stuffing with a spoon.

1 Put the chicken on a large chopping board or serving plate with the breast side uppermost. Steadying the joint with a carving fork, cut the skin between the breast and one thigh joint and work downward

through the meat to the joint. Bend the leg outward to locate the thigh joint, then cut down through the joint to remove the first leg.

2 To remove the wing on the same side of the chicken, cut down through the corner of the breast to the wing joint. Flex the wing as you did for the leg to locate the joint, then cut down between the joint to remove the wing.

3 Working on the same side of the chicken, make thin diagonal cuts down the breast to slice the meat, using the fork to steady the joint and to help you to remove each slice.

4 Now that the breast has been sliced, separate the thigh and drumstick joints, then cut thin slices of meat off both joints that follow the direction of the bone.

under 200
calories

chicken burgers & tomato salsa

Calories per serving **135**
Serves **4**
Preparation time **15 minutes**,
  plus chilling
Cooking time **10 minutes**

1 **garlic clove**, crushed
3 **scallions**, finely sliced
1 tablespoon **pesto**
2 tablespoons chopped **mixed
  herbs**, such as parsley,
  tarragon, and thyme
12 oz **ground chicken**
2 **sundried tomatoes**, finely
  chopped
1 teaspoon **olive oil**

Tomato salsa

8 oz **cherry tomatoes**,
  quartered
1 **red chile**, seeded and finely
  chopped
1 tablespoon chopped **fresh
  cilantro**
grated zest and juice of **1 lime**

Mix together all the burger ingredients, except the oil.
Divide the mixture into four and form into patties. Cover
and chill for 30 minutes.

Combine all the salsa ingredients in a bowl.

Brush the patties with the oil and cook under a high
broiler or on a barbecue for about 3–4 minutes each
side, until cooked through.

Serve each burger in a bread roll with the tomato salsa
and salad greens.

**For chile & cilantro chicken burgers with mango
salsa**, make the burgers as above. replacing the
sundried tomatoes with a finely chopped red chile
(and using cilantro pesto in place of the standard
pesto). Accompany with a salsa made from 1 large
mango, 1 small red onion, 1 red chile, 2 tablespoons
cilantro, and 2 tablespoons mint leaves, all finely
chopped and mixed with the juice of 1 lime and
2 teaspoons olive oil. **Calories per serving 191**

asian citrus chicken skewers

Calories per serving **143**
Serves **4**
Preparation time **5 minutes,**
  plus marinating
Cooking time **20 minutes**

1 lb boneless, skinless
  chicken breasts, cubed
grated zest and juice of 1
  lemon
2 teaspoons **Chinese 5-spice**
  powder
1 tablespoon **dark soy sauce**
mixed vegetables (carrots,
  scallions, radishes), cut into
  strips, to serve (optional)

Put the chicken, lemon zest and juice, 5-spice powder,
and soy sauce in a bowl. Stir to combine, cover, then
let marinate in the refrigerator for at least 1 hour or
overnight.

Thread the chicken pieces onto 4 presoaked wooden
skewers, pushing them tightly together. Broil for 10
minutes under a preheated moderate broiler. Turn the
skewers, baste with any remaining marinade, and broil
for another 10 minutes. Serve on a bed of vegetables,
if desired.

For piri piri chicken skewers, mix the grated lemon
zest and juice with 2 tablespoons olive oil, then add
2 teaspoons piri piri seasoning, 2 teaspoons tomato
paste and 2 cloves of finely chopped garlic. Add the
chicken, marinate, then broil as above. **Calories per**
serving 201

chicken & vegetable skewers

Calories per serving **149**
Serves **4**
Preparation time **10 minutes**
Cooking time **15 minutes**

4 **chicken thighs**, skinned and boned
2 tablespoons **honey**
2 tablespoons **mild wholegrain mustard**
1 **zucchini**, cut into 8 large pieces
1 **carrot**, cut into 8 large pieces

Cut the chicken thighs into bite-size pieces and toss in the honey and mustard, setting some aside for serving. Arrange the chicken pieces on a baking sheet and bake in a preheated oven, 350°F, for 15 minutes, until cooked through and lightly golden. Set aside and let cool.

Take 8 bamboo skewers and thread with the cooked chicken pieces and the raw vegetables.

Serve with the honey and mustard mixture for drizzling over. The skewers can also be refrigerated for adding to the following day's lunchbox.

For sticky chicken with honey & garlic, mix together 2 tablespoons ketchup, 2 teaspoons honey, 2 finely chopped cloves of garlic, and 1 tablespoon of sunflower oil. Dip the chicken into the ketchup mixture then cook as above. Thread onto skewers with 1 red bell pepper, seeded, cored, and cut into chunks and 8 halved cherry tomatoes. **Calories per serving 158**

miso chicken broth

Calories per serving **163**
Serves **4**
Preparation time **10 minutes**
Cooking time **16–18 minutes**

1 tablespoon **sunflower oil**
2 boneless, skinless **chicken breasts**, diced
8 oz **cup mushrooms**, sliced
1 **carrot**, cut into thin matchsticks
¾ inch piece **ginger root**, grated
2 large pinches **dried pepper flakes**
2 tablespoons **brown rice miso paste**
¼ cup **mirin** or **dry sherry**
2 tablespoons **light soy sauce**
5 cups **water**
2 **bok choy**, thinly sliced
4 **scallions**, thinly sliced
¼ cup chopped **fresh cilantro**

Heat the oil in a saucepan, add the chicken, and fry for 4–5 minutes, stirring until golden. Add the mushrooms and carrot sticks, then the ginger, pepper flakes, miso, mirin or sherry, and soy sauce.

Pour on the water and bring to a boil, stirring. Simmer for 10 minutes.

Add the bok choy, scallions, and chopped cilantro and cook for 2–3 minutes, until the bok choy has just wilted. Spoon into bowls and serve.

For hot & sour chicken soup, fry the chicken in oil as above, add 1½ cups sliced mushrooms and 1 carrot, cut into matchsticks. Flavor with 2 finely chopped garlic cloves, 3 teaspoons red Thai curry paste, 1 tablespoon Thai fish sauce, and 2 tablespoons light soy sauce. Add 5 cups chicken stock, bring to a boil, and cook for 10 minutes. Add 1 cup sliced baby corns, ½ cup sliced snow peas, and scallions and cilantro as above. Cook for 2–3 minutes. Ladle into bowls and serve with lime wedges. **Calories per serving 155**

szechuan chicken

Calories per serving **183**
  (excluding noodles and
  mushrooms)
Serves **4**
Preparation time **5 minutes,**
  plus marinating
Cooking time **16–20 minutes**

3 tablespoons **soy sauce**
2 tablespoons **dry sherry**
1 teaspoon **rice vinegar**
1¼ inch piece **ginger root**,
  peeled and finely chopped
1 **garlic clove**, crushed
1 tablespoon **Chinese chile**
  paste
½ teaspoon **Szechuan**
  peppercorns, ground
1 tablespoon **dark sesame oil**
4 x 4 oz boneless, skinless
  chicken breasts
chopped **fresh cilantro**, to
  garnish

To serve (optional)
soba noodles
stir-fried oyster mushrooms

Mix together all the ingredients except the chicken
and cilantro in a shallow dish to make the marinade.
Add the chicken breasts, coat well with the marinade,
and let marinate at room temperature for 2 hours.

Heat a ridged grill pan (or ordinary skillet). Cook the
chicken for 8–10 minutes on each side and garnish
with cilantro. Serve with soba noodles and stir-fried
oyster mushrooms, if desired.

For sesame greens with black bean sauce, to
accompany the chicken, fry 2 tablespoons sesame
seeds in 1 teaspoon sunflower oil until lightly browned.
Add 1 tablespoon soy sauce, cover with a lid and take
off the heat. When the bubbling subsides, scoop the
seeds into a dish. Rinse 13 oz collard greens and thickly
slice, stir-fry in 1 tablespoon oil with 2 cloves finely
chopped garlic until just wilted. Mix in 3 tablespoons
store-bought black bean sauce. Serve sprinkled with
the seeds. **Calories per serving 124**

chicken noodle soup

Calories per serving **191**
Serves **4**
Preparation time **10 minutes**
Cooking time **12 minutes**

5 cups **chicken stock**

1 **star anise**

3 inch piece of **cinnamon
stick**, broken up

2 **garlic cloves**, finely chopped

2 tablespoons **Thai fish sauce**

8 **cilantro roots**, finely
chopped

4 teaspoons **light brown
sugar**

4 teaspoons **light soy sauce**

7 oz boneless, skinless
chicken breast, cut into
cubes

4 oz **green vegetables**, such
as spring cabbage, chard, or
bok choy, coarsely chopped

¾ cup **bean sprouts**

7 oz **straight-to-wok rice
noodles**

¾ cup **fresh cilantro**

Put the chicken stock, star anise, cinnamon stick, garlic,
fish sauce, cilantro roots, sugar, and soy sauce into a
large saucepan and bring slowly to a boil.

Add the chicken and simmer gently for 4 minutes. Add
the green vegetables and bean sprouts and simmer for
2 minutes.

Divide the noodles between 4 bowls, pour over the
soup and sprinkle the cilantro on top.

For coconut & chicken soup, replace 1¾ cups of
the chicken stock with 1¾ cups canned reduced-
fat coconut milk. Cook the stock, herbs and spices,
sugar and fish and soy sauces, and chicken as above,
simmering the green vegetables and bean sprouts for
2 minutes and adding 1 cup shredded snow peas for
the final 1 minute of cooking for extra crunch. Ladle into
warm serving bowls over noodles as above and garnish
with fresh cilantro. **Calories per serving 266**

chicken minestrone

Calories per serving **197**
Serves **4**
Preparation time **5 minutes**
Cooking time **10 minutes**

1 (14½ oz) can diced
  tomatoes
2½ cups **chicken stock**
4 oz cooked **chicken**, chopped
1 **zucchini**, chopped
1 cup **mixed frozen**
  vegetables
¾ cup **mini-pasta shapes**
1 tablespoon ready-made
  pesto
salt and **pepper**

Put the tomatoes, stock, chicken, zucchini, and frozen vegetables in a saucepan. Bring to a boil, stirring, then add the pasta shapes and simmer for 5 minutes, until the pasta is just tender.

Season with salt and pepper and stir in the pesto just before serving.

For vegetable chicken & rice, put 1 (14½ oz) can diced tomatoes in a saucepan with 7 oz chopped cooked chicken, 1 chopped zucchini, 1 cup frozen mixed vegetables, and ½ cup chicken stock and heat. Simmer for 5 minutes, add 1¼ cups long-grain rice, and simmer again, stirring occasionally, for 10 minutes or until the rice is cooked, adding a little boiling water if the mixture is too dry. Stir in 2½ cups baby spinach leaves until just wilted. **Calories per serving 201**

smoked chicken bruschetta

Calories per serving **195**
Serves **4**
Preparation time **10 minutes**
Cooking time **10 minutes**

½ **ciabatta loaf**, cut into
  ½ inch slices
4 teaspoons **olive oil**
1 **garlic clove**, crushed
2 **scallions**, finely chopped
4 **ripe tomatoes**, finely
  chopped
1 tablespoon chopped **basil**
1 tablespoon **balsamic
  vinegar**
1 **smoked cooked chicken
  breast**, torn into small pieces
salt and **pepper**

Place the bread slices on a baking sheet. Mix together the oil and garlic and brush over the bread. Bake in a preheated oven, 350°F, for 10 minutes, until crisp.

Meanwhile, mix together the scallions, tomatoes, basil, and balsamic vinegar. Season with salt and pepper, then toss in the chicken pieces.

Spoon the tomato mixture onto the toasts to serve.

For smoked chicken toasts, combine the tomato and scallion as above and spread over French toast or store-bought Krisp rolls. Top with sliced smoked chicken and basil leaves. **Calories per serving 171**

under 300
calories

tandoori chicken salad

Calories per serving **200**
Serves **4**
Preparation time **15 minutes,**
  plus marinating
Cooking time **10 minutes**

¾ cup plain **yogurt**
2 tablespoons **lemon juice**
½ teaspoon **ground turmeric**
1 teaspoon **garam masala**
1 teaspoon **cumin** seeds,
  coarsely crushed
2 tablespoons **tomato paste**
2 **garlic cloves**, finely chopped
¾ inch piece of **fresh ginger
  root**, finely chopped
3 boneless, skinless **chicken
  breasts**, thickly sliced
1 tablespoon **sunflower oil**

Salad
5½ cups mixed **salad greens**
small bunch of **fresh cilantro**
4 tablespoons **lemon juice**

Mix the yogurt, lemon juice, spices, tomato paste, garlic, and ginger together in a shallow nonmetallic dish. Add the chicken and toss to coat. Cover and chill for 3–4 hours or until required.

When ready to serve, heat the oil in a large skillet, lift the chicken out of the marinade and add a few pieces at a time to the pan, until all the chicken is in the pan. Cook over a medium heat for 8–10 minutes, until the chicken is browned and cooked through.

Meanwhile, toss the salad greens and cilantro with the lemon juice and divide among serving plates. Spoon the chicken on top and serve immediately.

For tandoori chicken skewers, thread 12 oz chopped chicken breast onto 8 wooden skewers. Place in a large shallow ceramic dish and spoon over the yogurt marinade as above. When ready to serve, lift out of the marinade and cook under a hot broiler, turning occasionally until the chicken is cooked through. Serve with salad dressed with lemon juice as above.
Calories per serving 185

chicken & spinach curry

Calories per serving **205**
  (excluding rice)
Serves **4**
Preparation time **10 minutes**
Cooking time **25–30 minutes**

1 tablespoon **vegetable oil**
4 boneless, skinless **chicken
  breasts**, about 4 oz each,
  halved lengthwise
1 **onion**, sliced
2 **garlic cloves**, chopped
1 **green chile**, chopped
4 **cardamom pods**, lightly
  crushed
1 teaspoon **cumin seeds**
1 teaspoon **dried red pepper
  flakes**
1 teaspoon **ground ginger**
1 teaspoon **ground turmeric**
5 cups baby **spinach leaves**
1 ½ cups **tomatoes**
²/₃ cup **low-fat Greek yogurt**
2 tablespoons chopped fresh
  fresh cilantro, plus extra
  sprigs to garnish
boiled rice, to serve (optional)

Heat the oil in a large skillet or wok, add the chicken, onion, garlic, and chile and fry for 4–5 minutes or until the chicken begins to brown and the onion to soften. Add the cardamoms, cumin seeds, pepper flakes, ginger, and turmeric and fry for another 1 minute.

Add the spinach, cover, and cook gently until the spinach wilts, then stir in the tomatoes, replace the lid, and simmer for 15 minutes or until the chicken is cooked through, removing the lid for the last 5 minutes of cooking.

Stir the yogurt and cilantro into the curry and garnish with sprigs of cilantro. Serve with boiled rice, if desired.

deviled chicken

Calories per serving **207**
Serves **4**
Preparation time **10 minutes**
Cooking time **16–20 minutes**

8 small to medium, **boneless chicken thighs**
salad greens, to serve

For the devil sauce
2 tablespoons **Dijon mustard**
6 drops **Tabasco sauce**
2 **garlic cloves**, crushed
1 tablespoon **soy sauce**

Heat a large ridged grill pan (or ordinary skillet). Remove the skin from the chicken thighs, open them out and trim away any fat.

To make the devil sauce, mix together the mustard, Tabasco, garlic, and soy sauce in a shallow dish.

Dip the trimmed chicken thighs in the devil sauce and coat each piece well. Place the chicken pieces flat on the pan and cook for 8–10 minutes on each side.

Serve hot or cold with salad greens.

For jerk chicken, mix 3 tablespoons jerk marinade (a store-bought paste) with the grated zest and juice of ½ orange and 2 finely chopped cloves of garlic. Dip the chicken in this mixture then cook as above. Serve with rice or a salad. **Calories per serving 203**

chicken mulligatawny

Calories per serving **208**
  (excluding pappadams)
Serves **6**
Preparation time **15 minutes**
Cooking time **about 1 ¼ hours**

2 tablespoons **olive oil**
1 **onion**, finely chopped
1 **carrot**, diced
1 **dessert apple**, peeled,
  cored, and diced
2 **garlic cloves**, finely chopped
8 oz **tomatoes**, skinned if
  desired, coarsely chopped
4 teaspoons **medium curry
  paste**
⅓ cup **golden raisins**
½ cup **red lentils**
6 cups **chicken stock**
4 oz **leftover cooked chicken**,
  cut into shreds
salt and **pepper**
fresh cilantro sprigs, to
  garnish
pappadams, to serve
  (optional)

Heat the oil in a saucepan, add the onion and carrot and fry for 5 minutes, stirring until softened and just turning golden around the edges. Stir in the apple, garlic, tomatoes, and curry paste and cook for 2 minutes.

Stir in the raisins, lentils, and stock. Season with salt and pepper and bring to a boil, cover, and simmer for 1 hour, until the lentils are soft. Mash the soup to make a coarse puree. Add the cooked chicken, heat thoroughly then taste and adjust the seasoning if needed. Ladle into bowls and garnish with cilantro sprigs. Serve with pappadams, if desired.

For citrus carrot mulligatawny, fry the onion with 2½ cups diced carrots in 2 tablespoons sunflower oil for 5 minutes. Omit the next five ingredients, then add the red lentils, the grated zest and juice of 1 orange and ½ lemon, and 6 cups vegetable stock. Bring to a boil, cover, and simmer for 1 hour. Puree until smooth then reheat and adjust seasoning to serve. **Calories per serving 171**

chicken tikka sticks & fennel

Calories per serving **256**
Serves **4**
Preparation time **20 minutes,**
  plus marinating and chilling
Cooking time **8–10 minutes**

1 **onion**, finely chopped
½–1 large **red** or **green chile**,
  seeded and finely chopped
  (to taste)
¾ inch piece of **fresh ginger
  root**, finely chopped
2 **garlic cloves**, finely chopped
⅔ cup **fat-free plain yogurt**
3 teaspoons **mild curry paste**
¼ cup chopped **fresh cilantro**
4 **chicken breasts**, about
  5 oz each, cubed

Fennel raita
1 small **fennel bulb**, about
  7 oz
¾ cup **fat-free plain yogurt**
3 tablespoons chopped **fresh
  cilantro**
salt and **pepper**

Mix the onion, chile, ginger, and garlic together in a
shallow china or glass dish. Add the yogurt, curry paste,
and cilantro and mix together.

Add the cubed chicken to the yogurt mixture, mix
to coat, cover with plastic wrap and chill for at least
2 hours.

Make the raita. Cut the core away from the fennel and
finely chop the remainder, including any green tops.
Mix the fennel with the yogurt and cilantro and season
with salt and pepper. Spoon the raita into a serving dish,
cover with plastic wrap, and chill until needed.

Thread the chicken onto 12 skewers and place them
on a foil-lined grill rack. Cook under a preheated broiler
for 8–10 minutes, turning once, or until browned and
the chicken is cooked through. Transfer to serving
plates and serve with the raita on the side.

For a bell pepper & almond chutney, to serve with
the skewers instead of the raita, blend 1 cup store-
bought roasted peppers in a blender or food processor,
with a handful of mint leaves, 1 chopped garlic clove,
and ½ teaspoon chile powder. Blend until smooth, then
add salt to taste and 1 ½ tablespoons toasted sliced
almonds. Pulse a couple of times to coarsely crush
the almonds and stir in 1 tablespoon chopped cilantro.
Calories per serving 47

asian chicken cakes

Calories per serving **213**
   (excluding rice noodle
   salad)
Serves **4**
Preparation time **15 minutes**
Cooking time **16 minutes**

1 lb 3 oz **ground chicken**
1 **stalk lemon grass**, very
   finely chopped
2 **kaffir lime leaves**, very
   finely chopped
2 inch piece **ginger root**,
   peeled, very finely chopped
2 **green chiles**, very finely
   chopped
2 **garlic cloves**, very finely
   chopped
1 **egg**, beaten
1 tablespoon **sesame seeds**,
   toasted

To serve
sweet chili dipping sauce
rice noodle salad with
   chopped **peanuts**, sliced
   onion, **bean sprouts**, and
   chopped **fresh cilantro**
   (optional)

Put the chicken in a large bowl with the lemon grass, kaffir lime leaves, ginger, chiles, and garlic, which need to be so finely chopped as to almost make a paste. Add the beaten egg and sesame seeds. Mix well, using your hands.

Heat a ridged grill pan (or ordinary skillet). Divide the mixture into 16 and shape into small patties. Cook for 8 minutes on each side.

Serve the chicken cakes with sweet chili dipping sauce and a salad of rice noodles, chopped peanuts, sliced onion, bean sprouts and chopped cilantro, if desired.

For Chinese cabbage & bean sprout salad, as an alternative salad accompaniment, mix 1/4 cup sunflower oil, 2 tablespoons rice vinegar, 2 tablespoons light soy sauce, and 2 teaspoons fish sauce in a bowl. Add 1 1/3 sliced Chinese cabbage, 1 cup rinsed and drained bean sprouts, 4 sliced scallions, 8 oz carrots cut into matchstick strips, 1/3 cup coarsely chopped salted peanuts, and 2 tablespoons chopped mint, then toss together. **Calories per serving 247**

peppered chicken skewers

Calories per serving **216**
Serves **4**
Preparation time **10 minutes,**
   plus marinating
Cooking time **10 minutes**

4 boneless, skinless **chicken
   breasts**, about 5 oz each
2 tablespoons finely chopped
   rosemary, plus extra to
   garnish
2 **garlic cloves,** finely chopped
3 tablespoons **lemon juice**
2 teaspoons **mustard**
1 tablespoon **honey**
2 teaspoons freshly **ground
   black pepper**
1 tablespoon **olive oil**
pinch of **salt**
lemon wedges, to serve

Lay a chicken breast between 2 sheets of plastic wrap
and flatten slightly with a rolling pin or meat mallet.
Repeat with the remaining chicken breasts, then cut the
chicken into thick strips.

Put the chicken strips in a nonmetallic bowl and add
the remaining ingredients. Mix well, then cover and let
marinate in the refrigerator for 5–10 minutes.

Thread the chicken strips onto 8 skewers and cook
under a preheated medium-hot broiler for 4–5 minutes
on each side or until the chicken is cooked through.
Garnish with rosemary, and serve immediately with
lemon wedges.

For chicken & sweet chili sesame skewers, cut
1 lb chicken breasts into cubes, put in a small bowl,
drizzle with 2 teaspoons olive oil, and season with salt
and pepper. Thread onto skewers and cook under a
preheated hot broiler, turning occasionally until cooked
through. Remove from the heat and coat the skewers
with 2 tablespoons sweet chili sauce and sprinkle with
1 tablespoon sesame seeds. Cook under the broiler for
another minute on each side or until glazed. Serve with
a green salad. **Calories per serving 197**

greek chicken avgolomeno

Calories per serving **218**
Serves **6**
Preparation time **10 minutes**
Cooking time **15–20 minutes**

2 quarts **chicken stock**
1 cup **orzo**, **macaroni**, or
   other **small pasta shapes**
2 tablespoons **butter**
¼ cup **all-purpose flour**
4 **egg yolks**
grated zest and juice of
   1 **lemon**
salt and **pepper**

To garnish
4 oz cooked **chicken**, torn into
   fine shreds
extra **lemon zest**
oregano leaves
lemon wedges

Bring the stock to a boil, add the pasta, and simmer for 8–10 minutes, until just tender. Meanwhile heat the butter in a separate smaller pan, stir in the flour then gradually mix in 2 ladlefuls of the stock from the large pan. Bring to a boil, stirring. Take off the heat.

Mix the egg yolks in a medium-size bowl with the lemon zest and some salt and pepper. Gradually mix in the lemon juice until smooth. Slowly mix in the hot sauce from the small pan, stirring continuously.

Stir a couple more hot ladlefuls of stock into the lemon mixture once the pasta is cooked, then pour this into the large pasta pan. (Dont be tempted to add the eggs and lemon straight into the pasta pan or it may curdle.) Mix well, then ladle into shallow soup bowls and top with shredded chicken taken off the carcass, some extra lemon zest, and some torn oregano leaves. Serve with lemon wedges.

For green bean & asparagus salad, as an accompaniment, put 2 cups trimmed fine green beans in the top of a steamer, cover, and cook for 3 minutes. Add 13 oz trimmed fresh asparagus and cook for 5 minutes, until the vegetables are just tender. Mix together 5 tablespoons olive oil and 1 tablespoon each tapenade and balsamic vinegar and season. Drizzle over 2½ cups arugula leaves to serve. **Calories per serving 141**

ginger & honey chicken

Calories per serving **218**
  (excluding noodles)
Serves **4**
Preparation time **15 minutes,**
  plus soaking
Cooking time **10–15 minutes**

1 tablespoon **vegetable oil**
3 boneless, skinless **chicken**
  breasts, chopped
3 **chicken livers**, chopped
1 **onion**, finely sliced
3 **garlic cloves**, crushed
2 tablespoons **dried black**
  fungus (cloud's ears),
  soaked in hot water for
  20 minutes, then drained
2 tablespoons **light soy sauce**
1 tablespoon **honey**
2 tablespoons finely chopped
  fresh ginger root
5 **scallions**, chopped
1 **red chile**, seeded and finely
  sliced into strips, to garnish
rice noodles, to serve
  (optional)

Heat the oil in a wok over medium heat and add the chicken breasts and livers. Fry the chicken mixture for 5 minutes, then remove it using a slotted spoon and set aside.

Add the onion to the wok and fry it over low heat until soft. Remove half the onions from the wok and set aside. Add the garlic and the drained mushrooms and stir-fry for 1 minute. Return the chicken mixture to the wok.

Stir together the soy sauce and honey in a bowl until blended, then pour this over the chicken and stir well. Add the ginger and stir-fry for 2–3 minutes. Finally, add the scallions and garnish with the reserved onions and strips of red chile. Serve immediately with medium rice noodles, if desired.

For ginger and honey chicken with bok choy, cook as in the main recipe, adding 1 head shredded bok choy or ½ head shredded Chinese cabbage to the wok with the ginger and serve without noodles.
Calories per serving 196

low-fat lemon chicken

Calories per serving **219**
  (excluding rice)
Serves **4**
Preparation time **12 minutes**,
  plus marinating
Cooking time **8 minutes**

1 **egg**, lightly beaten
2 **garlic cloves**, sliced
2 small pieces of **lemon** peel,
  plus juice of 1 lemon
1 lb boneless, skinless
  chicken breasts, cut into
  ¼ inch slices
2 tablespoons **cornstarch**
1 tablespoon **canola** or
  olive oil
1 **scallion**, diagonally sliced
  into ¾ inch lengths
lemon slices, to garnish
boiled rice, to serve (optional)

Mix the egg, garlic, and lemon peel together in a shallow dish, add the chicken and let marinate for 10–15 minutes.

Remove the lemon peel and add the cornstarch to the marinated chicken. Mix thoroughly to distribute the cornstarch evenly among the chicken slices.

Heat the oil in a wok over high heat until the oil starts to shimmer. Add the chicken slices, making sure you leave a little space between them, and fry for 2 minutes on each side.

Reduce the heat to medium and stir-fry for 1 more minute or until the chicken is browned and cooked. Turn up the heat and pour in the lemon juice. Add the scallion, garnish with lemon slices, and serve immediately with rice, if desired.

For warm lemon chicken & herb salad, cook the chicken as above, then toss into a bowl with ½ sliced cucumber, a handful of cilantro, 6 torn basil leaves and 1¼ cups wild arugula. Dress the salad lightly with ½ teaspoon sesame oil and 1 teaspoon canola or olive oil. **Calories per serving 242**

spiced chicken & mango salad

Calories per serving **222**
Serves **4**
Preparation time **15 minutes**
Cooking time **5–6 minutes**

4 small boneless, skinless
  chicken breasts
6 teaspoons **mild curry paste**
juice of 1 **lemon**
²/₃ cup **low-fat plain yogurt**
1 **mango**
1 ¼ cups **watercress**
½ **cucumber**, diced
½ **red onion**, chopped
½ **iceberg lettuce**

Cut the chicken breasts into long, thin slices. Put 4 teaspoons of the curry paste in a plastic bag with the lemon juice and mix together by squeezing the bag. Add the chicken and toss together.

Half-fill the base of a steamer with water and bring to a boil. Place the chicken in the top of the steamer in a single layer, cover, and steam for 5–6 minutes, until thoroughly cooked. Test the chicken to make sure it is cooked.

Meanwhile, mix the remaining curry paste in a bowl with the yogurt.

Cut a thick slice off either side of the mango to reveal the large, flat pit. Trim the flesh away from the pit, then remove the peel and cut the flesh into bite-size chunks.

Rinse the watercress with cold water and tear it into bite-size pieces. Add to the yogurt dressing with the cucumber, red onion, and mango and toss together gently.

Tear the lettuce into pieces, divide it among 4 plates, spoon the mango mixture on top, and complete with the warm chicken strips.

For coronation chicken, mix the curry paste and yogurt with ¼ cup reduced-fat mayonnaise. Stir in 1 lb cold cooked diced chicken and ¼ cup golden raisins. Sprinkle with ¼ cup toasted sliced almonds and serve on a bed of mixed salad and herb leaves. **Calories per serving 338**

caribbean chicken skewers & salsa

Calories per serving **236**
 (excluding rice)
Serves **4**
Preparation time **30 minutes,**
 plus marinating
Cooking time **10–12 minutes**

4 tablespoons **pineapple
 juice** (from can below)
1 tablespoon **ketchup**
1 teaspoon **paprika**
½ teaspoon **ground cinnamon**
large pinch **ground allspice**
4 boneless, skinless **chicken
 breasts**, cubed
1 **red bell pepper**, cored,
 seeded, cut into chunks
1 **orange bell pepper**, cored,
 seeded, cut into chunks
boiled rice, to serve (optional)

For the salsa
1 (7½ oz) can **pineapple rings
 in natural juice**, drained
2 **tomatoes**, diced
½ cup frozen **corn kernels**,
 just thawed
½ **red chile**, seeded, finely
 chopped (optional)
¾ inch piece **ginger root**,
 finely chopped
fresh cilantro, coarsely chopped

Put the pineapple juice into a bowl. Stir the ketchup and
spices into the juice, add the chicken and toss together.
Let marinate for at least 30 minutes.

Meanwhile, to make the salsa, finely chop the
pineapple rings and put in a bowl with the tomatoes
and corn. Add the chile (if using), ginger, and half the
cilantro and toss together.

Thread the chicken pieces, then the pepper chunks,
onto 12 wooden or metal skewers. Sprinkle the skewers
with the remaining chopped cilantro. Broil the skewers
under a preheated hot broiler for 10–12 minutes,
turning several times until well browned and the chicken
is cooked through.

Serve the skewers with spoonfuls of the salsa and
rice, if desired.

For Caribbean rice salad, put 1 cup easy-cook
brown rice in a saucepan of boiling water and cook for
25–30 minutes or until tender. Drain the rice, rinse well
with cold water, then drain again. Mix it with the salsa,
5–7 oz diced cooked chicken, ¼ cup toasted shredded
coconut, and 1 seeded and diced red bell pepper.
Calories per serving 400

chicken & asparagus salad

Calories per serving **244**
Serves **2**
Preparation time **10 minutes**
Cooking time **5 minutes**

5 oz **asparagus**, cut into 2
    inch lengths
7 oz **smoked chicken breast**
½ cup **cherry tomatoes**,
    halved
1 (10 oz) can **cannellini
    beans**, drained and rinsed
handful of **chives**, chopped

Dressing
2 tablespoons **olive oil**
2 teaspoons **honey**
2 teaspoons **balsamic vinegar**
2 teaspoons **whole-grain
    mustard**
1 **garlic clove**, crushed

Cook the asparagus in a large saucepan of lightly
salted boiling water for about 4 minutes or until just
tender. Drain and plunge into cold water to prevent
more cooking. Pat dry with kitchen towels.

Cut the chicken into bite-size pieces and transfer
them to a large salad bowl. Add the tomatoes, beans,
asparagus, and chopped chives and mix well.

Make the dressing by whisking the oil, honey, vinegar,
and mustard with the crushed garlic in a small bowl.
Pour the dressing over the salad and toss well to coat.

For chicken, asparagus, & haloumi salad, prepare
2½ oz asparagus as above and set aside. Heat a
ridged grill pan and cook 2 chicken breasts, each about
5 oz, for 5–6 minutes on each side or until cooked. Set
aside, cover with foil, and keep warm. Cut 4 oz haloumi
cheese into ¼ inch slices and fry for 2 minutes on each
side until golden and crispy. Mix ½ teaspoon Dijon
mustard, 1 ½ tablespoons lemon juice, 2 tablespoons
olive oil, and 1 tablespoon coarsely chopped tarragon in
a small bowl. Slice the chicken and arrange on serving
plates with the haloumi and asparagus. Drizzle over the
dressing and serve. **Calories per serving 480**

chicken, tarragon, & orange salad

Calories per serving **246**

Serves **4**

Preparation time **20 minutes**, plus chilling

Cooking time **1¼–1½ hours**, plus reduction and thinning

3 lb **whole chicken**

1 medium **onion**, thinly sliced

grated zest and juice of

 1 orange

1 tablespoon chopped **fresh tarragon** (or 1 teaspoon dried)

1 **bay leaf**

1 tablespoon **olive oil**

½–1 tablespoon **white wine vinegar**

salt and **pepper**

To garnish

1 small **orange**, thinly sliced

small bunch **garden and cress**

tarragon sprigs (optional)

Put the chicken, onion, orange zest and juice, tarragon, and bay leaf in a large saucepan. Pour enough water over the top of the chicken to cover it and sprinkle with salt and pepper to taste. Cover, bring to a boil, and simmer for 1–1¼ hours, until the chicken is cooked.

Lift the chicken out of the saucepan and let cool. Discard the bay leaf and onion. Measure the stock, then boil until it reduces to ⅔ cup. Set aside to cool, then chill in the refrigerator.

When the chicken is cold, take the meat off the bones, discarding the skin. Cut the meat into bite-size pieces and place in a bowl.

When the stock has chilled, remove the layer of fat from the top, then reheat gently to thin it. Stir in the oil, add the vinegar, and season to taste. Pour this dressing over the chicken and toss well.

Serve immediately, garnished with orange slices, garden, cress, and tarragon sprigs, if desired, or cover and chill until required. The salad may also be served on a bed of shredded iceberg lettuce.

For chicken, tarragon, & orange tagliatelle, add ½ cup half-fat sour cream to the cooled and reduced stock. Stir in the diced chicken, then reheat. Add ½ cup torn watercress and cook for 1 minute, until the leaves just wilt. Toss with just-cooked tagliatelle (approximately 5 oz per person). **Calories per serving 496**

64

asian chicken parcels

Calories per serving **247**
  (excluding jasmine rice)
Serves **4**
Preparation time **5 minutes**
Cooking time **15 minutes**

4 **boneless, skinless chicken breasts**, about 200 g (7 oz) each
75 ml (3 fl oz) **light soy sauce**
1 tablespoon **clear honey**
2 **garlic cloves**, sliced
2 **red chillies**, deseeded and finely chopped
2.5 cm (1 inch) piece of **fresh root ginger**, peeled and finely shredded
4 **star anise**
3 **baby pak choi**, quartered
jasmine rice, to serve
  (optional)

Score each chicken breast several times with a knife and put one on each of 4 x 12 inch squares of foil.

Combine the soy sauce, honey, garlic, chiles, ginger, and star anise in a small bowl, then spoon over the chicken.

Arrange 3 bok choy quarters on top of the chicken breasts. Seal the edges of the foil together to form parcels, transfer to a baking sheet, and bake in a preheated oven, 400°F, for 15 minutes, until the chicken is cooked through.

Let rest for 5 minutes, then serve the parcels with boiled jasmine rice, if desired.

For Mediterranean chicken parcels, score the chicken breasts as above, put on the foil squares and season with salt and pepper. Top with 2 teaspoons dried oregano, 2 chopped tomatoes, 1/3 cup chopped pitted black ripe olives, 2 tablespoons drained capers in brine, and a good drizzle of extra virgin olive oil. Cook in the oven as above. **Calories per serving 277**

nasi goring

Calories per serving **255**
Serves **4**
Preparation time **10 minutes**
Cooking time **10 minutes**

2 tablespoons **vegetable oil**
5 oz boneless, skinless
  chicken breast, finely
  chopped
2 oz cooked peeled **shrimp**,
  defrosted if frozen
1 **garlic clove**, crushed
1 **carrot**, shredded
¼ **white cabbage**, thinly
  sliced
1 **egg**, beaten
2¼ cups cold cooked **basmati
  rice**
2 tablespoons **ketchup manis**
  (sweet soy sauce)
½ teaspoon **sesame oil**
1 tablespoon **chili sauce**
1 **red chile**, seeded and cut
  into strips, to garnish

Heat the oil in a wok or large skillet, add the chicken
and stir-fry for 1 minute. Add the shrimp, garlic, carrot,
and cabbage and stir-fry for 3–4 minutes.

Pour in the egg and spread it out using a wooden
spoon. Cook until set, then add the rice and break up
the egg, stirring it in.

Add the ketchup manis, sesame oil, and chili sauce
and heat through. Serve immediately, garnished with
the chile strips.

For vegetarian nasi goring, crush a garlic clove and
stir-fry it in 2 tablespoons oil with 1 chopped carrot
and ¼ chopped white cabbage. Omit the chicken and
shrimp but add 1 finely sliced red bell pepper, 3 cups
sliced shiitake mushrooms, and 2 heads finely shredded
bok choy. Stir-fry for another 2–3 minutes, until the
vegetables are soft yet still retaining their shape. Add
the remaining ingredients and serve in warm serving
bowls. **Calories per serving 225**

peppered chicken & eggplant

Calories per serving **256**
  (excluding salad and
  bread)
Serves **4**
Preparation time **15 minutes**
Cooking time **15 minutes**

2 tablespoons **sunflower oil**
6 boneless, skinless **chicken**
  thighs, cut into cubes
1 large **eggplant**, diced
1 **red onion**, sliced
2 **garlic cloves**, finely chopped
2 tablespoons **medium hot**
  curry paste
½ teaspoon **black**
  peppercorns, coarsely
  crushed
small bunch **fresh cilantro**, to
  garnish

To serve (optional)
tomato salad
bread

Heat the oil in a large skillet, add the chicken and eggplant and fry, stirring for 5 minutes, until the eggplant is just beginning to soften. Stir in the onion and garlic and fry for 5 more minutes, stirring until the onion and chicken are just beginning to brown.

Mix in the curry paste and peppercorns and fry for 5 minutes, until the chicken is a rich golden brown and cooked through when tested (see page 15). Tear the cilantro into pieces and sprinkle over the top. Serve immediately with bowls of tomato salad and warmed bread, if desired.

For curried chicken with mixed vegetables, use a small eggplant rather than a large one, then mix in 1 diced zucchini and 1 diced and seeded green bell pepper along with the onion. Finish with 2 cups spinach and cook for 2 minutes, until just wilted. **Calories per serving 270**

chicken satay

Calories per serving **257**
Serves **6**
Preparation time **10 minutes,**
  plus marinating
Cooking time **10 minutes**

2 tablespoons smooth **peanut
  butter**
½ cup **soy sauce**
½ cup **lime juice**
2 tablespoons **curry powder**
2 **garlic cloves**, chopped
1 teaspoon **hot pepper sauce**
6 boneless, skinless **chicken
  breast**s, cubed

To serve (optional)
lemon wedges

Combine the peanut butter, soy sauce, lime juice, curry powder, garlic, and hot pepper sauce in a nonmetallic dish. Add the chicken, mix well, and chill for 12 hours or until required.

When ready to serve, divide the chicken cubes among 6 metal skewers and cook under a preheated hot broiler for 5 minutes on each side, until tender and cooked through. Serve immediately with lemon wedges, if desired.

For miso-broiled chicken, mix 2 tablespoons each soy sauce, dry sherry or rice wine, and 2 teaspoons clear honey and miso paste. Add the cubed chicken and marinate as above. Thread onto skewers and cook as above. Serve with rice and a sliced cucumber and red chile salad. **Calories per serving 224**

72

crispy spiced chicken wings

Calories per serving **260**
Serves **4 as an appetizer**
Preparation time **5 minutes**
Cooking time **18 minutes**

1 cup **all-purpose flour**
1 tablespoon **hot chile
  powder**
½ teaspoon **salt**
12 **chicken wings**
vegetable oil, for deep-frying
1 **red chile** sliced into thin
  rounds
3 **scallions**, thinly sliced
1 tablespoon finely chopped
  fresh ginger root
lime wedges, to serve

Put the flour, chile powder, and salt in a large bowl and combine thoroughly. Add the chicken wings and toss well to coat in the flour.

Pour enough oil into a wok to deep-fry the chicken, and heat it to 375°F, or until a cube of bread dropped into the oil turns golden in 20 seconds. Deep-fry 6 chicken wings for 6–7 minutes, turning them in the oil until golden and crisp, then remove using a slotted spoon and drain on kitchen towels. Fry the remaining chicken wings in the same way.

Lower the chile, scallions, and ginger into the oil, using a slotted spoon, and sizzle until crisp and the chile is a vibrant red. Drain thoroughly on paper towels.

Pile the chicken wings onto a serving plate. Sprinkle with the crispy chile, scallions, and ginger and serve with the lime wedges.

For sweet chili dip, to serve with the chicken wings, cut 3 slices from a cucumber and finely chop. Stir into a bowl with 1 tablespoon chopped cilantro, the grated zest of 1 lime, and 1 teaspoon Thai fish sauce (nam pla). Stir in 5 tablespoons sweet chili sauce. **Calories per serving 65**

bhoona chicken curry

Calories per serving **262**
Serves **4**
Preparation time **10 minutes,**
 plus marinating
Cooking time **8–10 minutes**

½ cup **fat-free plain yogurt**
juice of 2 **limes**
2 **garlic cloves**, finely chopped
1 teaspoon **ground turmeric**
1 tablespoon **mild chile**
 powder
1 teaspoon **cardamom seeds**,
 crushed
large pinch of **sea salt**
1 tablespoon **ground cilantro**
1 tablespoon **ground cumin**
4 boneless, skinless **chicken**
 breasts, cut into strips
1 tablespoon **peanut oil**
1 teaspoon **garam masala**
handful of coarsely chopped
 fresh cilantro
steamed rice, to serve
 (4 tablespoons per serving)

Put the yogurt, lime juice, garlic, turmeric, chile powder, cardamom, salt, ground cilantro, and cumin in a large nonmetallic bowl. Mix well and add the chicken. Toss to coat evenly, cover, and marinate in the refrigerator for 6–8 hours or overnight.

Heat the oil in a large nonstick skillet over medium-high heat, and stir-fry the chicken mixture for 8–10 minutes, until tender and cooked through.

Sprinkle with the garam masala and chopped cilantro, stir well, and serve with steamed rice.

For masala chicken kebabs, prepare the marinade as above and add 4 boneless, skinless chicken breasts, cut into cubes. Marinate in the refrigerator for 6–8 hours or overnight if time permits. When ready to cook, thread the chicken pieces onto 8 metal skewers and cook under a medium-hot broiler for 5–6 minutes on each side or until cooked through. Serve with warmed naan bread or rice. **Calories per serving 234**

kung po chicken

Calories per serving **266**
Serves **4**
Preparation time **5 minutes**
Cooking time **10 minutes**

2 tablespoons **peanut oil**
2–3 **red chiles**, deseeded and
  sliced
2 **garlic cloves**, finely chopped
13 oz boneless, skinless
  chicken breasts, cut into
  ½ inch cubes
1 teaspoon **chile bean sauce**
½ cup canned sliced **bamboo
  shoots**, drained
½ cup canned **water
  chestnuts**, drained
1 tablespoon **Chinese rice
  wine** or **dry sherry**
½ cup **chickenstarch** or **water**
1 teaspoon **cornflour** mixed
  to a paste with 1 tablespoon
  water
¼ cup **roasted unsalted
  peanuts**
2 **scallions**, cut into ½ inch
  lengths

Heat the oil in a wok over high heat until the oil starts
to shimmer. Add the chiles and garlic and stir-fry for a
few seconds.

Add the chicken and chile bean sauce and stir-fry for
a couple of minutes, then add the bamboo shoots,
water chestnuts, rice wine, and stock and bring to a boil.
Slowly add the cornstarch paste, stirring until the sauce
has thickened and turned transparent.

Stir the peanuts and scallions into the dish just before
serving.

For coconut rice, to serve with Kung Po Chicken,
put 1 cup washed Thai jasmine or long-grain rice in
a saucepan and add 3 tablespoons full-fat coconut
milk. Pour in water to a level of 1 inch above the rice.
Bring to a boil, then lower the heat to a slow simmer.
Cover with a tightly fitting lid, cook for 10 minutes,
then turn off the heat and let the rice steam in the
pan for another 10 minutes before serving. **Calories
per serving 204**

chicken livers with green beans

Calories per serving **269**
Serves **4 as an appetizer**
Preparation time **15 minutes**
Cooking time **8 minutes**

1 lb **chicken livers**
5 tablespoons **peanut oil**
3 **shallots**, very thinly sliced
½ teaspoon finely sliced **fresh
  ginger root**
2 **garlic cloves**, finely sliced
1 **green chile**, very thinly
  sliced
¾ cup **green beans**, cut into
  ½ inch slices
½ teaspoon **sugar**
1 tablespoon **malt vinegar**
1 tablespoon **Chinese rice
  wine** or **dry sherry**
2 tablespoons **oyster sauce**
2 handfuls of shredded
  iceberg lettuce
salt and **black pepper**
dried red pepper flakes, to
  serve

Trim away any white membrane on the chicken livers
and pat the livers dry with paper towels. Lightly season
with salt and pepper and set aside.

Heat the oil in a wok over high heat until the oil starts
to shimmer. Add the shallots and give them a quick stir,
then add the ginger, garlic, and chile. Fry until crisp but
not too dark, then remove using a slotted spoon and
drain on paper towels.

Toss in half the chicken livers and cook over high heat
for 1 minute on each side, until just browned. Set aside
and fry the remaining livers in the same way, adding
some more oil to the wok if needed.

Return all the livers to the wok, then toss in the
beans and stir-fry for 1 minute. Stir in the remaining
ingredients and continue cooking until the livers are well
coated in a rich sauce.

Spoon onto a serving dish with the shredded lettuce
and spoon the crispy shallot mixture over the top. Serve
with a small bowl of dried red pepper flakes on the side.

For warm chicken liver salad, cook the livers as
above, then toss into a bowl with 2 cups watercress,
approximately 10 cucumber slices, and 1 tablespoon
toasted sesame seeds. Serve as an appetizer or light
lunch. **Calories per serving 290**

aromatic chicken pancakes

Calories per serving **269**
Serves **4**
Preparation time **10 minutes**
Cooking time **7 minutes**

4 boneless, skinless **chicken breasts**, about 5 oz each
6 tablespoons **hoisin sauce**

To serve
12 **Chinese pancakes**, warmed
½ **cucumber**, cut into matchsticks
12 **scallions**, thinly sliced
handful of **fresh cilantro**
¼ cup **hoisin sauce** mixed with 3 tablespoons **water**

Lay a chicken breast between 2 sheets of plastic wrap and flatten with a rolling pin or meat mallet until it is 1 inch thick. Repeat with the remaining chicken breasts. Transfer to a baking sheet and brush with some of the hoisin sauce.

Cook the chicken breasts under a preheated hot broiler for 4 minutes. Turn them over, brush with the remaining hoisin sauce and cook for another 3 minutes or until the chicken is cooked through.

Meanwhile, warm the pancakes in a bamboo steamer for 3 minutes or until heated through.

Slice the chicken thinly and arrange it on a serving plate. Serve with the pancakes, accompanied by the cucumber, scallions, cilantro, and diluted hoisin sauce in separate bowls, so that everyone can assemble their own pancakes.

For satay chicken pancakes, in a nonmetallic dish mix together 6 tablespoons dark soy sauce, 2 tablespoons sesame oil, and 1 teaspoon Chinese five-spice powder, add the flattened chicken breasts and coat evenly with the marinade. Cover and let marinate in the refrigerator. Put ¼ cup peanut butter, 1 tablespoon dark soy sauce, ½ teaspoon cumin powder, ½ teaspoon ground cilantro, a pinch of paprika, and ½ cup water in a saucepan and mix together over low heat. Transfer to 4 small bowls. Cook the chicken and pancakes as above and serve with the satay sauce. **Calories per serving 411**

one-pot chicken

Calories per serving **275**
Serves **4**
Preparation time **10 minutes**
Cooking time **45 minutes**

1 lb **new potatoes**
4 **chicken breasts**, about
   4 oz each
6 tablespoons **mixed herbs**,
   such as **parsley, chives,**
   chervil, and **mint**
1 **garlic clove**, crushed
6 tablespoons **half-fat sour**
   cream
8 **baby leeks**
2 **endive** heads, halved
   lengthways
²/₃ cup **chicken stock**
pepper

Put the potatoes in a saucepan of boiling water and cook for 12–15 minutes, until tender. Drain, then cut into bite-size pieces.

Make a slit lengthwise down the side of each chicken breast to form a pocket, ensuring that you do not cut all the way through. Mix together the herbs, garlic, and sour cream, season well with pepper, then spoon a little into each chicken pocket.

Put the leeks, endives, and potatoes in an ovenproof dish. Pour over the stock, then lay the chicken breasts on top. Spoon over the remaining sour cream mixture, then bake in a preheated oven, 400°F, for 25–30 minutes.

For baked chicken with fennel & potatoes, cut the potatoes in half and place them in a large ovenproof dish with 1 large fennel bulb, cut into quarters. Omit the leeks and endive. Pour over the stock and bake in a preheated oven, 400°F, for 20 minutes. Remove from the oven and lay the chicken breasts over the vegetables. Combine 1 tablespoon chopped parsley with 1 tablespoon Dijon mustard and the half-fat sour cream, omitting the garlic, and spoon the mixture over the chicken. Bake for another 25–30 minutes. **Calories per serving 271**

corn & chicken chowder

Calories per serving **284**
Serves **6**
Preparation time **15 minutes**
Cooking time **about 30 minutes**

2 tablespoons **butter** or **margarine**
1 large **onion**, chopped
1 small **red bell pepper**, cored, seeded, and diced
1¼ lb **potatoes**, diced
¼ cup **all-purpose flour**
3 cups **chicken stock**
¾ cup **canned** or **frozen corn kernels**
8 oz **cooked chicken**, chopped
1¾ cups **low-fat milk**
3 tablespoons chopped **parsley**
salt and **pepper**
a few sliced **red chiles**, to garnish

Melt the butter or margarine in a large saucepan. Add the onion, bell pepper, and potatoes and fry over moderate heat for 5 minutes, stirring from time to time.

Sprinkle in the flour and cook over gentle heat for 1 minute. Gradually stir in the stock and bring to a boil, stirring. Lower the heat, cover the pan and cook for 10 minutes.

Stir in the corn, chicken, and milk. Season to taste with salt and pepper, cover the pan, and simmer gently for another 10 minutes, until the potatoes are just tender. Taste and adjust the seasoning if necessary. Serve the chowder garnished with the sliced chiles and parsley.

For spicy corn chowder, fry the onion, bell pepper, and potato in the butter as above with 4 finely chopped red chiles. Add the flour then stir in the stock and simmer for 10 minutes. Stir in the corn and milk, season and simmer as above until the potatoes are just tender. Garnish with cilantro sprigs. **Calories per serving 194**

seared chicken sandwich

Calories per serving **293**
Serves **4**
Preparation time **15 minutes**
Cooking time **5–6 minutes**

8 oz **mini chicken breasts**
8 teaspoons **balsamic vinegar**
8 slices **wholegrain bread**
6 tablespoons **low-fat plain yogurt**
½–1 teaspoon **freshly grated hot horseradish** or **horseradish sauce**, to taste
3 cups **mixed salad greens with beet strips**
pepper

Put the mini chicken breasts into a plastic bag with half the vinegar and toss together until evenly coated.

Heat a nonstick skillet, lift the chicken out of the plastic bag with a fork, and add the pieces to the pan. Fry for 3 minutes, turn and drizzle with the vinegar from the bag and cook for 2–3 more minutes or until browned and cooked through.

Toast the bread lightly on both sides. Slice the chicken into long, thin strips. Mix together the yogurt and horseradish and a little pepper to taste. Add the salad leaves and toss together.

Arrange the yogurt and salad leaves on 4 slices of toast, then add some chicken strips, drizzle over the remaining vinegar, if desired, and top with the remaining slices of toast. Cut each sandwich in half and serve immediately.

For tangy chicken, lemon, & garlic toasties, toss the chicken breasts with the juice of ½ lemon and 1 tablespoon olive oil, then fry as above but without the vinegar. Toast 8 slices whole-wheat bread, then spread with ¼ cup reduced-fat garlic mayonnaise. Divide the chicken among 4 slices of toast, then top with the shredded leaves of 2 small crisphead lettuces and a 2 inch piece of cucumber, thinly sliced. Cover with the remaining slices of toast, then press together and cut into triangles. **Calories per serving 320**

gingered chicken with soft noodles

Calories per serving **297**
Serves **4**
Preparation time **10 minutes**
Cooking time **12–13 minutes**

2 teaspoons **sesame oil**
2 teaspoons **sunflower oil**
2 boneless, skinless **chicken breasts**, diced
2 **garlic cloves**, finely chopped
1 inch piece **ginger root**, peeled, finely grated
10 oz package **ready-prepared stir-fry crunchy vegetables**
¼ cup **ready-salted peanuts**, coarsely chopped
13 oz pack **chilled fresh egg noodles**
2 tablespoons **sweet chili dipping sauce**
3 tablespoons **soy sauce**
2 teaspoons **fish sauce** (optional)
small bunch **fresh cilantro**, to garnish (optional)

Pour the oils into a wok or large skillet. When hot, add the chicken and stir-fry for 5 minutes, until lightly browned. Add the garlic and ginger and cook for 1 minute.

Add the mixed vegetables and stir-fry for 3 minutes. Mix in the peanuts and the noodles and stir-fry for 2–3 minutes, until hot. Add the chili sauce, soy sauce, and fish sauce, if using, and cook for 1 minute. Spoon into small bowls, and garnish with torn cilantro, if desired.

For gingered chicken with bean sprout salad, fry the chicken as above, omitting the stir-fried vegetables and noodles, then let cool. Mix 1 cup rinsed bean sprouts with 1 finely shredded romaine lettuce, 1 carrot, and 1 zucchini, both coarsely grated. Add the chicken, peanuts, and sauces and toss together. Garnish with torn cilantro. **Calories per serving 233**

under 400 calories

chicken with leek & asparagus

Calories per serving **301**
Serves **4**
Preparation time **10 minutes**
Cooking time **12 minutes**

1 teaspoon **cornstarch**
1 teaspoon **dark soy sauce**
2 tablespoons **water**
1 tablespoon **sugar**
1 tablespoon **malt vinegar**
3 tablespoons **peanut oil**
1¼ lb boneless, skinless
   chicken breasts, cut into
   thin strips
1 tablespoon chopped **fresh
   ginger root**
large pinch of **dried red
   pepper flakes**
1 **leek**, thinly sliced
10 oz **asparagus**, halved
   length- and widthwise
salt and **white pepper**
boiled rice, to serve (optional)

Mix the cornstarch and soy sauce to make a smooth paste, then add the water, sugar, and malt vinegar. Set aside.

Heat half the oil in a wok over high heat until the oil starts to shimmer. Add the chicken strips and season with salt and white pepper. Stir-fry for 3–4 minutes, until golden, then remove the chicken with a slotted spoon and set aside.

Return the wok to the heat and pour in the remaining oil. Add the ginger, pepper flakes, and leek and stir-fry over medium heat for 3–4 minutes, until the leeks have started to soften. Stir in the asparagus and cook for 1 minute.

Transfer the chicken back to the wok and cook for 1 minute. Pour in the cornstarch mixture and cook, stirring, until it becomes a thick and velvety sauce. Serve with rice, if desired.

For rice with leeks, ginger, & cumin, as an accompaniment, trim 2 large leeks and wash carefully. Drain them and slice into thin rounds. Heat 1 tablespoon olive oil in a large nonstick saucepan. Add 1 teaspoon grated ginger and 1 teaspoon cumin powder. Add the sliced leeks, season, and cook for around 10 minutes, stirring regularly. If necessary, add 1 or 2 tablespoons of water to keep the mixture from sticking. Season to taste. Add 3 cups cooked rice to the pan and fluff up the grains with a fork. **Calories per serving 176**

warm chicken salad with anchovies

Calories per serving **303**
Serves **4**
Preparation time **20 minutes**
Cooking time **15–17 minutes**

1¼ cup **green beans**, thickly
  sliced
1 small **crisp lettuce**, leaves
  separated and torn into
  pieces
6 **scallions**, thinly sliced
¾ cup **cherry tomatoes**,
  halved
1 (9 oz) jar **mixed pepper
  antipasto in oil**
2 boneless, skinless **chicken
  breasts**, diced
1 cup **fresh bread crumbs**
4 canned **anchovy fillets**,
  drained, chopped

For the dressing
3 tablespoons **olive oil**
2 teaspoons **tomato paste**
4 teaspoons **red wine vinegar**
salt and **pepper**

Blanch the green beans in a saucepan of boiling water
for 3–4 minutes, until just tender. Drain, rinse with cold
water, and drain again.

Put the beans, lettuce, scallions, and tomatoes into
a large salad bowl. Lift the peppers out of the jar,
reserving the oil, dice if needed and add to the salad.

Pour 2 tablespoons oil from the pepper jar into a skillet,
add the chicken and fry for 8–10 minutes, stirring until
golden and cooked through. Spoon over the salad. Heat
1 tablespoon extra oil in the pan, add the bread crumbs
and anchovies, and stir-fry until golden.

Mix the dressing ingredients together, toss over
the salad, then sprinkle with the bread crumbs and
anchovies and serve immediately.

For chicken Caesar salad, mix the green beans
with the lettuce, 4 hard-cooked eggs cut into wedges,
scallions and lettuce as above, plus 4 chopped
anchovy fillets. Cut 3 oz bread into cubes and fry in
2 tablespoons olive oil and 2 tablespoons butter. Set
the croutons aside and fry 2 chicken breasts in the
same pan, turning until golden and cooked through. Mix
¼ cup reduced-fat mayonnaise with 1 finely chopped
garlic clove and the juice of 1 lime. Toss with the
salad, then sprinkle with croutons and ⅓ cup grated
Parmesan cheese. **Calories per serving 346**

thai chicken curry

Serves **4**
Calories per serving **307**
Preparation time **5 minutes**
Cooking time **15 minutes**

1 tablespoon **sunflower oil**
1 tablespoon **Thai green
curry paste** (see below)
6 **kaffir lime leaves**, torn
2 tablespoons **Thai fish sauce**
1 tablespoon packed **light
brown sugar**
¾ cup **chicken stock**
1¾ cups **coconut milk**
1 lb boneless, skinless
chicken thigh fillets, diced
1 (4 oz) can **bamboo shoots**,
drained
1 (4 oz) can **baby corn**,
drained
large handful of **Thai basil
leaves** or **fresh cilantro**,
plus extra to garnish
1 tablespoon **lime juice**
1 **red chile**, seeded and
sliced, to garnish

Heat the oil in a wok or large skillet, add the curry paste and lime leaves and stir-fry over low heat for 1–2 minutes or until fragrant.

Stir in the fish sauce, sugar, stock, and coconut milk and bring to a boil, then reduce the heat and simmer gently for 5 minutes.

Add the chicken and cook for 5 minutes. Add the bamboo shoots and baby corn and cook for an additional 3 minutes or until the chicken is cooked through.

Stir through the basil or cilantro and lime juice, then serve garnished with the extra leaves and chile.

For homemade Thai green curry paste, put 15 small green chiles, 4 halved garlic cloves, 2 finely chopped lemon grass stalks, 2 torn Kaffir lime leaves, 2 chopped shallots, 1 inch piece of fresh ginger root, peeled and finely chopped, 2 teaspoons black peppercorns, 1 teaspoon pared lime zest, ½ teaspoon salt, and 1 tablespoon peanut oil in a food processor or blender and blend to a thick paste. Transfer to a screw-top jar. This makes about ⅔ cup of paste, which can be stored in the refrigerator for up to 3 weeks. **Calories per serving (1 tablespoon) 32**

teriyaki chicken with three seeds

Calories per serving **307**
Serves **4**
Preparation time **20 minutes,**
  plus marinating
Cooking time **16–20 minutes**

4 boneless, skinless **chicken
  breasts**, about 4 oz each
2 tablespoons **sunflower oil**
4 tablespoons **soy sauce**
2 **garlic cloves**, finely chopped
1 inch piece **fresh ginger
  root**, finely grated
2 tablespoons **sesame seeds**
2 tablespoons **sunflower
  seeds**
2 tablespoons **pumpkin
  seeds**
juice of 2 **limes**
1¼ cups **herb salad**
½ small **iceberg lettuce,**
torn into bite-size pieces
1½ cups **alfalfa** or **brocco
  sprouting seeds**

Put the chicken breasts into a shallow ceramic dish.
Spoon three-quarters of the oil over the chicken, then
add half the soy sauce, the garlic, and the ginger.

Turn the chicken to coat in the mixture, then leave to
marinate for 30 minutes.

Heat a nonstick skillet, then lift the chicken out of the
marinade and add to the pan. Fry for 8–10 minutes
each side, until dark brown and cooked all the way
through. Lift out and set aside.

Heat the remaining oil in the pan, add the seeds,
and fry for 2–3 minutes until lightly toasted. Add the
remaining marinade and remaining soy sauce, bring to
a boil, then take off the heat and mix in the lime juice.

Mix the herb salad, lettuce, and sprouting seeds
together, then spoon over 4 serving plates. Thinly slice
the chicken and arrange on top, then spoon the seed
and lime dressing over the top. Serve at once.

For teriyaki chicken with oriental salad, marinate
the chicken as above and make a salad with 7 oz
carrots, cut into thin strips, 4 scallions, cut into thin
strips, 6 thinly sliced radishes, and ½ small head of
Chinese cabbage, thinly shredded. Fry the chicken
as above, omit the seeds and then continue with the
dressing as above. Slice the chicken, arrange on the
salad and drizzle with the warm dressing. **Calories per
serving 289**

chicken fillets with soy glaze

Calories per serving **363**
Serves **4**
Preparation time **10 minutes,**
 plus chilling
Cooking time **30 minutes**

4 **chicken breasts**
4 tablespoons **dark soy sauce**
3 tablespoons packed **light
 brown sugar**
2 **garlic cloves**, crushed
2 tablespoons **white wine
 vinegar**
½ cup freshly squeezed
 orange juice
pepper

To serve
steamed vegetables such as
 broccoli
rice (1 tablespoon per serving)

Lay the chicken fillets on a chopping board and slice each in half horizontally. Place in a large, shallow ovenproof dish, in which the fillets fit snugly.

Mix together the soy sauce, sugar, garlic, vinegar, orange juice, and pepper and pour the mixture over the chicken. Cover and chill the dish until you are ready to cook it.

Uncover the dish and bake the chicken in a preheated oven, 350°F, for 30 minutes, until it is cooked through. Transfer to serving plates and spoon the cooking juices over the meat.

Serve with steamed vegetables and rice (1 tablespoon per person).

For chicken breasts with oriental glaze, lay 4 boneless, skinless chicken breasts in a shallow ovenproof dish. Combine the ingredients for the dressing as above, omitting the orange juice and adding 2 teaspoons chopped ginger and 2 tablespoons Chinese cooking wine or dry sherry. Cook in a preheated oven, 400°F, for 15 minutes, then serve with a sprinkling of cilantro, steamed vegetables, and rice. **Calories per serving 359**

warm chicken & pine nut salad

Calories per serving **319**
Serves **4**
Preparation time **10 minutes**
Cooking time **15 minutes**

¼ cup **pine nuts**
4 boneless, skinless **chicken breasts**, halved horizontally
2–3 teaspoons **paprika**
1 tablespoon **olive oil**
handful of **radicchio leaves**
2½ cups **mixed salad greens**
1 **red onion**, thinly sliced
¼ cup **sherry vinegar**
2 teaspoons **Dijon mustard**
2 tablespoons **honey**
⅓ cup **raisins**
salt and **pepper**

Heat a nonstick skillet until hot. Add the pine nuts and dry-fry, stirring continuously, until golden, taking care not to let them burn. Transfer them from the pan to a plate.

Lightly dust the chicken breast halves with paprika and season with salt and pepper. Heat the oil in the pan and fry the chicken breasts, turning occasionally, for about 10 minutes or until cooked through.

Meanwhile, mix together the radicchio, salad greens, and red onion and place on serving plates. Remove the chicken from the pan and stir the vinegar, mustard, and honey into the pan juices. Heat though and add the raisins and pine nuts. Pour the warm dressing over the salad and serve with the chicken.

For chicken, raisin, & pine nut pilau, cook 1¼ cups basmati rice in lightly salted boiling water for 10 minutes or according to the instructions on the package. Cut 4 boneless, skinless chicken breasts into bite-size pieces and fry in 1 tablespoon olive oil and 1 teaspoon smoked paprika with 1 thinly sliced red onion for 5 minutes. Add the drained rice with 2½ cups baby spinach leaves, 2 tablespoons raisins, and 2 tablespoons pine nuts. Season and stir well to mix. **Calories per serving 463**

red chicken & coconut broth

Calories per serving **322**
Serves **4**
Preparation time **10 minutes**
Cooking time **20–21 minutes**

1 tablespoon **sunflower oil**
8 oz boned and skinned
  chicken thighs, diced
4 teaspoons store-bought **red
  Thai curry paste**
1 teaspoon store-bought
  galangal paste
3 **dried kaffir lime leaves**
1¾ cups **coconut milk**
2 teaspoons **Thai fish sauce**
1 teaspoon **light brown sugar**
2½ cups **chicken stock**
4 **scallions**, thinly sliced, plus
  2 extra to garnish
½ cup **snow peas**, sliced
1 cup **bean sprouts**, rinsed
small bunch of **fresh cilantro**

Heat the oil in a saucepan, add the chicken and curry paste and fry for 3–4 minutes, until just beginning to color. Stir in the galangal paste, lime leaves, coconut milk, fish sauce, and brown sugar, then mix in the stock.

Bring to a boil, cover, and simmer for 15 minutes, stirring occasionally until the chicken is cooked.

Create curls by cutting very thin strips from the two scallions reserved for a garnish. Soak in cold water for 10 minutes, then drain.

Add the remaining scallions, snow peas, and bean sprouts to the pan, and cook for 2 minutes. Ladle into bowls and tear the cilantro over the top. Sprinkle the scallion curls over the soup.

For veggie Thai broth, heat the oil, add the curry paste, and fry for 1 minute. Add the galangal paste, lime leaves, coconut milk, fish sauce, and brown sugar. Pour in ¾ cup vegetable stock then add 1 cup baby corn finely sliced with the snowpeas. Cover and simmer for 10 minutes. Serve with the cilantro as above. **Calories per serving 268**

chicken ratatouille

Calories per serving **333**
Serves **2**
Preparation time **15 minutes**
Cooking time **25 minutes**

2 tablespoons **olive oil**
2 boneless, skinless **chicken
   breasts**, cut into bite-size
   pieces
½ cup thinly sliced **zucchini**
⅓ cup cubed **eggplant**
1½ cups thinly sliced **onion**
⅓ cup thinly sliced **green bell
   pepper**
1 cup sliced **mushrooms**
1 (14½ oz) can **plum
   tomatoes**
2 **garlic cloves**, finely chopped
1 teaspoon organic **vegetable
   bouillon powder**
1 teaspoon **dried basil**
1 teaspoon **dried parsley**
½ teaspoon **ground black
   pepper**

Heat the oil in a large skillet, add the chicken and cook, stirring, for 3–4 minutes, until browned all over. Add the zucchini, eggplant, onion, bell pepper, and mushrooms and cook, stirring occasionally, for 15 minutes or until tender.

Add the tomatoes to the pan and gently stir. Stir in the garlic, bouillon powder, herbs, and pepper and simmer, uncovered, for 5 minutes or until the chicken is tender. Serve immediately.

chicken teriyaki

Calories per serving **340**
Serves **4**
Preparation time **5 minutes,**
  plus marinating
Cooking time **5–6 minutes**

4 boneless, skinless **chicken
  breasts**, about 1 lb in total, cut
  into 1 inch cubes
¼ cup **dark soy sauce**, plus
  extra to serve
¼ cup **mirin**
2 tablespoons **sugar**
8 oz **cooked soba noodles**
3 tablespoons **sesame oil**

Put the chicken in a shallow dish. Combine the soy sauce, mirin, and sugar, add to the chicken and toss well to coat. Set aside to marinate for 15 minutes.

Meanwhile, cook the noodles according to the package instructions, then drain, refresh in iced water, drain again and chill.

Thread the chicken cubes onto metal skewers and broil or grill for 2–3 minutes on each side.

Toss the noodles with a little sesame oil and serve with the chicken and the remaining sesame oil and soy sauce.

For chicken teriyaki with beans & cilantro, cut 4 boneless, skinless chicken breasts into cubes and place in a nonmetallic dish. Make the marinade as above and marinate the cubed chicken in the mixture for 15 minutes. Thinly slice and blanch 1 cup green beans. Toss the cooked beans with 1 tablespoon sesame oil and a large handful of fresh cilantro. Thread the chicken cubes onto skewers and cook under a preheated broiler, turning occasionally until cooked through. Serve the skewers with the cooled beans and cilantro. **Calories per serving 297**

tandoori chicken skewers

Calories per serving **343**
Serves **4**
Preparation time **10 minutes,**
plus marinating
Cooking time **about 10
minutes**

¾ cup **fat-free plain yogurt**
3 tablespoons **tandoori
powder**
1 tablespoon finely grated
garlic
1 tablespoon peeled and finely
grated **fresh ginger root**
juice of **2 limes**
2 lb boneless, skinless
chicken breasts, cubed
2 **yellow bell peppers,** cored,
seeded, and cubed
2 **red bell peppers,** cored,
seeded, and cubed
salt and **pepper**

To serve (optional)
naan bread

Put the yogurt, tandoori powder, garlic, ginger, and lime
juice in a large nonmetallic bowl. Mix well, season to
taste, and add the chicken. Toss to coat evenly, cover, and
marinate in the refrigerator for 6–8 hours or overnight.

Preheat the broiler to medium-hot. Thread the chicken
onto 8 metal skewers, alternating with the pepper
pieces, and broil for 4–5 minutes on each side, until
the edges are lightly charred and the chicken is cooked
through. Serve with the pomegranate raita (see below),
or warmed naan breads, if desired.

For pomegranate raita, to serve as an accompaniment,
put 1 ¼ cups fat-free plain yogurt in a bowl. Coarsely
grate ½ cucumber, squeeze out the excess liquid
and add to the yogurt with a small handful of finely
chopped mint leaves, 2 teaspoons lightly dry-roasted
cumin seeds, and ¾ cup pomegranate seeds. Season,
mix well, and chill until ready to serve. **Calories per
serving 19**

griddled salsa chicken

Calories per serving **343**
Serves **4**
Preparation time **10 minutes**
Cooking time **6 minutes**

4 **boneless chicken breasts**,
   skin on
3 tablespoons **olive oil**
salt and **pepper**

**For the cucumber & tomato
salsa**
1 **red onion**, finely chopped
2 **tomatoes**, seeded and
   diced
1 **cucumber**, finely diced
1 **red chile**, finely chopped
small handful of fresh **cilantro**,
   chopped
juice of **1 lime**

Remove the skin from the chicken breasts. Using
kitchen scissors, cut each breast in half lengthwise
but without cutting the whole way through. Open each
breast out flat. Brush with the oil and season well with
salt and pepper. Heat a ridged grill pan until very hot.
Add the chicken breasts and cook for 3 minutes on
each side or until cooked through and grill-marked.

Meanwhile, to make the salsa, mix together the onion,
tomatoes, cucumber, red chile, cilantro and lime juice.
Season well with salt and pepper.

Serve the chicken hot with the spicy salsa spooned
over and around.

For pineapple salsa, as an accompaniment,
mix together 6 tablespoons drained and roughly
diced canned pineapple, 1 finely chopped red onion,
1 tablespoon finely chopped fresh ginger root, 1 finely
chopped red chile, grated zest and juice of 1 lime,
2 teaspoons honey, and salt and pepper to taste.
Calories per serving 38

bamboo chicken with cashews

Calories per serving **343**
(excluding rice)
Serves **4**
Preparation time **10 minutes**
Cooking time **15 minutes**

1 cup **chicken stock**
13 oz boneless, skinless
  chicken breasts, cubed
2 tablespoons **yellow bean
  sauce**
1 cup sliced **carrots**
1½ cups canned sliced
  bamboo shoots, drained
1 teaspoon **cornstarch**
  mixed to a paste with 2
  tablespoons **water**
1 cup **cashew nuts**, toasted
1 **scallion**, shredded
boiled rice, to serve (optional)

Heat the chicken stock in a wok. Add the chicken meat and bring the stock back to a boil, stirring, then lower the heat and cook for 5 minutes. Remove the chicken using a slotted spoon and set aside.

Add the yellow bean sauce to the wok and cook for 2 minutes. Add the carrots and bamboo shoots and cook for another 2 minutes.

Return the chicken to the pan, bring the sauce back to a boil and thicken with the cornstarch paste. Stir in the cashews and scallion just before serving. Serve with rice, if desired.

For mild chicken curry with peanuts, cook the chicken as above. Replace the yellow bean sauce with ½ tablespoon mild Madras paste and cook for 2 minutes, then add the carrot with 1 cup broccoli florets instead of the bamboo shoots. Continue the recipe as above, finishing by stirring in ⅔ cup chopped roasted peanuts in place of the cashews and 2 sliced scallions. **Calories per serving 350**

chicken kofta curry

Calories per serving **343**
Serves **4**
Preparation time **15 minutes**
Cooking time **25 minutes**

1 ½ lb **ground chicken**
2 teaspoons peeled and finely
   grated **fresh ginger root**
2 **garlic cloves**, crushed
2 teaspoons **fennel seeds**,
   crushed
1 teaspoon **ground cinnamon**
1 teaspoon **chili powder**
cooking oil spray
2 cups **tomato sauce with
   onions and garlic**
1 teaspoon **ground turmeric**
2 tablespoons **medium curry
   powder**
1 teaspoon **agave syrup**
salt and **pepper**

To serve
½ cup **fat-free plain yogurt**,
   whisked
pinch of **chili powder**
chopped **mint leaves**

Put the chicken in a bowl with the ginger, garlic, fennel seeds, cinnamon, and chili powder. Season to taste and mix thoroughly with your hands until well combined. Form the mixture into walnut-size balls.

Spray a large nonstick skillet with cooking oil spray and place over medium heat. Add the chicken balls and stir-fry for 4–5 minutes or until lightly browned. Transfer to a plate and keep warm.

Pour the tomato sauce into the skillet and add the turmeric, curry powder, and agave syrup. Bring to a boil, then reduce the heat to a simmer, season to taste and carefully place the chicken balls in the sauce. Cover and cook gently for 15–20 minutes, turning the balls occasionally, until they are cooked through.

Serve immediately, drizzled with the yogurt and sprinkled with chili powder and mint leaves.

For quick chunky chicken Madras, replace the ground chicken with cubed, boneless, skinless chicken breasts and the medium curry powder with Madras curry powder. Cook as above and add 2 cups peas for the last 5 minutes of cooking. Serve hot. **Calories per serving 387**

smoked mustard chicken

Calories per serving **345**
Serves **4**
Preparation time **10 minutes**
Cooking time **20 minutes**

1 tablespoon **whole-grain mustard**
1 tablespoon **extra virgin olive oil**
4 **chicken breasts**, about 6 oz each
¾ cup uncooked **rice**
1 cup **Earl Grey tea leaves**
salt and **black pepper**
steamed vegetables, such as broccoli, to serve

For the salsa verde
handful of **flat-leaf parsley**
handful of **mint leaves**
handful of **basil leaves**
1 teaspoon **capers**
2 **anchovies** in oil
1 **garlic clove**, crushed
¼ cup **olive oil**
1 tablespoon **red wine vinegar**

Stir together the mustard and olive oil and season with salt and pepper. Rub this mixture all over the chicken breasts and set aside.

Prepare a wok for smoking by lining it with foil, then add the rice and tea leaves, mixed together. Put a circular rack in the wok and place the wok over high heat with the lid on. Heat until smoke starts to escape out of it.

Remove the lid and quickly sit the chicken on the rack. Replace the lid and cook for 3 minutes, then reduce the heat to medium and cook for another 10 minutes. Turn the heat off and let the chicken sit in the wok for 5 minutes more while you prepare the salsa verde.

Blend all the salsa verde ingredients in a mini food processor or chop them up finely by hand. Transfer to a bowl and adjust the seasoning to taste. Serve the chicken warm or at room temperature with the salsa verde on the side and steamed vegetables such as tenderstem broccoli.

For fennel, lemon, & honey smoked chicken, season 2 tablespoons honey with salt and pepper and smear all over 4 chicken breasts. Prepare the wok for smoking as above, using the contents of 10 fennel tea bags instead of the Earl Grey and adding the zest of 2 lemons to the mixture. Cook the chicken as above. **Calories per serving 337**

chicken & bok choy noodles

Calories per serving **345**
Serves **4**
Preparation time **10 minutes**,
  plus marinating
Cooking time **7 minutes**

1 lb boneless, skinless
  chicken breasts, cut into
  thin strips
1 tablespoon **Chinese rice
  wine** or **dry sherry**
2 teaspoons **cornstarch**
½ teaspoon **sesame oil**
½ teaspoon **salt**
2 tablespoons **peanut oil**
5 **scallions**, cut into
  1 inch lengths
1 inch piece **fresh ginger
  root**, cut into matchsticks
1 **red chile**, seeded and thinly
  sliced
1 tablespoon **sesame seeds**
3 heads of **bok choy**, cut into
  2 inch pieces
2 tablespoons **oyster sauce**
1 tablespoon **water**
10 oz **straight-to-wok
  noodles**

Put the chicken in a bowl with the rice wine, cornstarch,
sesame oil, and salt and let marinate for 30 minutes.

Heat the oil in a wok over high heat until the oil starts
to shimmer. Add the chicken strips, scallions, ginger,
chile, and sesame seeds and stir-fry for 2 minutes
before adding the bok choy. Stir for 1 minute, then add
the oyster sauce and measured water. Cook, stirring,
for 1 minute, then toss in the noodles and stir-fry until
steaming hot.

For chicken & shrimp noodles, follow the recipe as
above, but with 10½ oz of chicken and adding 5 oz
cooked small shrimp to the pan with the bok choy.
Calories per serving 329

cashew chicken with peppers

Calories per serving **348**
  (excluding rice)
Serves **4**
Preparation time **10 minutes**
Cooking time **15 minutes**

2 tablespoons **peanut oil**
1¼ lb boneless, skinless
  chicken breasts, cut into
  1 inch pieces
⅓ cup **cashew nuts**
2 **red bell peppers**, cored,
  seeded, and cut into large
  pieces
2 **garlic cloves**, chopped
6 **scallions**, halved widthwise
  and lengthwise
salt
boiled rice, to serve (optional)

Sauce
1 tablespoon **Chinese rice
  wine** or **dry sherry**
1 teaspoon **sesame oil**
2 tablespoons **light soy sauce**
½ teaspoon **cornstarch**
¼ cup **water**

Combine all the ingredients for the sauce and set the mixture aside.

Heat 1 tablespoon of the peanut oil in a wok over high heat until the oil starts to shimmer. Season the chicken with salt and put half of it into the wok. Stir-fry for 2–3 minutes, until golden, then remove the chicken using a slotted spoon and set aside. Heat the remaining oil and stir-fry the rest of the chicken in the same way. Remove and set aside.

Add the cashews and bell peppers to the wok and stir-fry for 1 minute. Add the garlic and scallions and cook, stirring, for another minute. Return the chicken to the wok and pour in the sauce. Cook for 3–4 minutes, until the chicken is cooked through and the pepper is tender. Serve with rice, if desired.

For cashew chicken with peppers & water chestnuts, add 8 halved water chestnuts to the wok with the peppers in the third step. After 1 minute add the garlic and the scallions, cook for 1 minute, then return the chicken and add the sauce to the pan as described above. Stir in ¾ cup bean sprouts 1 minute before the end of cooking. **Calories per serving 359**

124

thai sesame chicken patties

Calories per serving **349**
Serves **4**
Preparation time **15 minutes,**
    plus chilling
Cooking time **10 minutes**

4 **scallions**
1 cup **fresh cilantro**, plus extra
    to garnish
1 lb **ground chicken**
3 tablespoons **sesame seeds**,
    toasted
1 tablespoon **light soy sauce**
1 ½ inch piece of **fresh ginger
    root**, peeled and finely
    grated
1 **egg white**
1 tablespoon **sesame oil**
1 tablespoon **sunflower oil**
**Thai sweet chili dipping
    sauce**, to serve
    (approximately 2 tablespoons
    per person)
scallion curls, to garnish
    (optional)

Chop the scallions and cilantro finely in a food
processor or with a knife. Put in a bowl and mix with
the chicken, sesame seeds, soy sauce, ginger, and
egg white.

Divide the mixture into 20 mounds on a chopping
board, then shape into slightly flattened rounds with
wetted hands. Chill in the refrigerator for 1 hour (or
longer if you have time).

Heat the sesame and sunflower oils in a large skillet,
add the patties and fry for 10 minutes, turning once or
twice, until golden and cooked through to the center.

Arrange on a serving plate with a small bowl of chili
dipping sauce in the center. Garnish with extra cilantro
and scallion curls, if desired.

For baby leaf stir-fry with chili, to serve as an
accompaniment, heat 2 teaspoons sesame oil in the
same pan used to cook the patties. Add an 8 oz pack
of store-bought baby leaf and baby vegetable stir-
fry ingredients and stir-fry for 2–3 minutes until the
vegetables are hot. Mix in 2 tablespoons light soy sauce
and 1 tablespoon Thai sweet chili dipping sauce. Serve
in a side bowl with the chicken patties. **Calories per
serving 55**

chicken mole

Calories per serving **351**
Serves **4**
Preparation time **25 minutes**
Cooking time **50 minutes**

1 tablespoon **sunflower oil**
1 lb **ground chicken**
1 **onion**, coarsely chopped
2 **garlic cloves**, finely chopped
1 teaspoon **smoked paprika**
½ teaspoon **dried chile seeds**
1 teaspoon **cumin seeds**,
  roughly crushed
1 (14½ oz) can **diced
  tomatoes**
1 (15 oz) can **red kidney
  beans**
²/₃ cup **chicken stock**
1 tablespoon packed **dark
  brown sugar**
2 oz **dark chocolate**, diced
salt and **pepper**

Heat the oil in a saucepan, add the chicken and onion and fry, breaking up the chicken with a wooden spoon until browned. Mix in the garlic, paprika, chile, and cumin seeds and cook for 1 minute.

Stir in the tomatoes, beans, stock, and sugar, then mix in the chocolate and seasoning. Cover and simmer gently for 45 minutes, stirring occasionally. Spoon the mole into bowls to serve

chicken with orange & mint

Calories per serving **355**
Serves **4**
Preparation time **5 minutes**
Cooking time **15–20 minutes**

salt and **pepper**
4 boneless, skinless **chicken breasts**, about 7 oz each
3 tablespoons **olive oil**
2/3 cup freshly squeezed **orange juice**
1 **small orange**, sliced
2 tablespoons chopped **mint**
1 tablespoon **butter**
couscous (approximately 2 tablespoons per serving), to serve (optional)

Season the chicken breasts to taste with salt and pepper. Heat the oil in a large nonstick skillet, add the chicken breasts and cook over medium heat, turning once, for 4–5 minutes or until golden all over.

Pour in the orange juice, add the orange slices, and bring to a gentle simmer. Cover tightly, reduce the heat to low, and cook gently for 8–10 minutes or until the chicken is cooked through. Add the chopped mint and butter and stir to mix well. Cook over high heat, stirring, for 2 minutes. Serve with couscous, if desired.

For chicken with rosemary & lemon, bruise 4 sprigs of rosemary in a mortar and pestle, then chop finely. Put the grated zest and juice of 2 lemons, 3 crushed garlic cloves, ¼ cup olive oil, and the rosemary in a nonmetallic dish. Add the chicken breasts and mix to coat thoroughly. Cover and let marinate in the refrigerator until required. Cook the chicken breasts in a preheated hot ridged grill pan for 5 minutes on each side or until cooked through. **Calories per serving 370**

grilled summer chicken salad

Calories per serving **357**
Serves **4**
Preparation time **15 minutes**
Cooking time **45 minutes**

4 x 4 oz boneless, skinless
  chicken breasts
2 small **red onions**
2 **red bell peppers**, cored,
  seeded, cut into flat pieces
1 bunch of **asparagus**,
  trimmed
7 oz **new potatoes**, boiled,
  cut in half
bunch of **basil**
5 tablespoons **olive oil**
2 tablespoons **balsamic**
  vinegar
salt and **pepper**

Heat a ridged grill pan (or ordinary skillet). Place the chicken breasts in the pan and cook for 8–10 minutes on each side. When cooked, remove from the pan and chop into chunks.

Cut the red onions into wedges, keeping the root ends intact to hold each wedge together. Place in the pan and cook for 5 minutes on each side. Remove from the pan and set aside.

Place the flat pieces of bell pepper in the pan and cook for 8 minutes on the skin side only, so that the skins are charred and blistered. Remove and set aside, then cook the asparagus in the pan for 6 minutes, turning frequently.

Put the boiled potatoes in a large bowl. Tear the basil, reserving a few leaves intact to garnish, and add to the bowl, together with the chicken and all the vegetables. Add the olive oil, balsamic vinegar, and seasoning. Toss the salad and garnish with the reserved basil leaves.

For summer chicken wraps, omit the potatoes and follow the recipe as above. Warm 4 soft tortillas as directed on the pack, then spread with 2/3 cup reduced-fat hummus. Toss the grilled chicken (torn into strips) and the vegetables with 2 tablespoons olive oil, the balsamic vinegar, and reserved basil leaves as above. Divide between the tortillas, then roll up tightly and serve cut in half while the chicken is still warm. **Calories per serving 489**

broiled gazpacho chicken salad

Calories per serving **359**
Serves **4**
Preparation time **10 minutes**
Cooking time **10–12 minutes**

6 tablespoons **olive oil**
¼ cup finely chopped **basil**
3 **chicken breasts**, each
about 5 oz
1 (14 oz) jar **piquante
peppers** (5½ oz drained)
1 bunch of **scallions**, coarsely
chopped
1¼ cups **cucumber** chopped
coarsely
8 oz **cherry plum tomatoes**,
halved
¼ cup chopped **flat-leaf
parsley**

Put 2 tablespoons of the oil in a shallow bowl with
3 tablespoons of the basil. Brush the mixture over
the chicken breasts. Place the chicken on a foil-lined
broiler rack and cook under a preheated hot broiler for
5–6 minutes on each side or until golden and
cooked through.

Meanwhile, put the piquante peppers in a large salad
bowl with the scallions, cucumber, cherry tomatoes, and
parsley and toss together. Add the remaining oil and
basil and toss again.

Cut the hot chicken into thin slices and toss into the
salad and serve.

For gazpacho soup with chicken salsa, put 4 quartered
tomatoes in a food processor or blender with 3 drained
piquante peppers, 4 chopped scallions, and 1¼ cups
coarsely chopped cucumber and process until thick and
smooth. Add 1 (14½ oz) can diced tomatoes and blend
again. Meanwhile, chop 1 cooked chicken breast, about
4 oz, into small pieces and mix with 1 tablespoon
chopped parsley. Ladle the cold soup into 4 serving bowls
and top each serving with a spoonful of chicken salsa.
Calories per serving 100

spiced roast chicken with lime

Calories per serving **362**
Serves **4**
Preparation time **15 minutes**
Cooking time **25–30 minutes**

8 small **chicken thighs**,
  skinned
1 tablespoon **harissa**
4 tablespoons **honey**
2 **limes**, cut into wedges
1 **red bell pepper**, cored,
  seeded, and cut into large
  chunks
2 **zucchini**, cut into chunks
1 **onion**, cut into wedges
10 oz **new potatoes**, halved
  if large
1 tablespoon **olive oil**
salt and **pepper**

Cut a few slashes across each chicken thigh. Mix together the harissa and honey and rub all over the chicken thighs. Place in a roasting pan large enough to spread everything out in a single layer, with the lime wedges, bell pepper, zucchini, onion, and potatoes.

Drizzle over the oil, season with salt and pepper and roast in a preheated oven, 425°F, for 25 minutes, turning occasionally, or until the chicken is cooked and the vegetables are tender. Serve with the juice of the lime wedges squeezed over the chicken.

For pan-fried spicy chicken, cut 8 small boneless, skinless chicken thigh fillets into strips and coat in a mixture of 1 tablespoon harissa and 1 tablespoon honey. Heat 1 tablespoon sunflower oil in a large skillet, add the chicken, and fry over medium heat for 5 minutes. Add 1 seeded and chopped bell pepper, 2 chopped zucchini, 1 onion, cut into thin wedges, and 2 limes, cut into wedges. Cook for 10 minutes, stirring occasionally, or until the chicken is cooked and the vegetables are tender. Serve with new potatoes.
Calories per serving 316

136

chicken, apricot, & almond salad

Calories per serving **366**
Serves **4**
Preparation time **15 minutes**

7 oz **celery**
½ cup **almonds**
3 tablespoons chopped
  parsley
¼ cup **mayonnaise**
3 poached or roasted **chicken
  breasts**, each about 5 oz
12 **fresh apricots**
salt and **pepper**

Thinly slice the celery sticks diagonally, reserving the yellow inner leaves. Transfer to a large salad bowl together with half the leaves. Coarsely chop the almonds and add half to the bowl with the parsley and mayonnaise. Season to taste with salt and pepper.

Arrange the salad on a serving plate. Shred the chicken and halve and pit the apricots. Add the chicken and apricots to the salad and stir lightly to combine.

Garnish with the remaining almonds and celery leaves and serve.

For grilled chicken with apricot & tomato salad, marinate 4 chicken breasts, each about 5 oz, with 2 crushed garlic cloves, 3 tablespoons sweet chili sauce, and the juice and zest of 1 lime for at least 1 hour. Remove the chicken from the marinade and transfer to a heated ridged grill pan. Cook until golden and cooked through. Remove the pits and chop 12 apricots into ¼ inch pieces. Mix with 3 ripe tomatoes cut into ¼ inch pieces and 2 tablespoons chopped cilantro. Whisk together 3 tablespoons red wine vinegar, 3 tablespoons olive oil, 1 teaspoon brown sugar, and 1 teaspoon soy sauce and pour the dressing over the salad. Combine well and serve with the chicken. **Calories per serving 331**

chicken with spring vegetables

Calories per serving **370**
Serves **4**
Preparation time **10 minutes,**
  plus resting
Cooking time **about 1¼ hours**

3 lb **whole chicken**
about 6 cups hot **chicken
  stock**
2 **shallots**, halved
2 **garlic cloves**
2 **parsley sprigs**
2 **marjoram sprigs**
2 **lemon thyme sprigs**
2 **carrots**, halved
1 **leek**, trimmed and sliced
7 oz **broccolini**
8 oz **asparagus**, trimmed
½ **Savoy cabbage**, shredded

Put the chicken in a large saucepan and pour over enough stock to just cover the chicken. Push the shallots, garlic, herbs, carrots, and leek into the pan and bring to a boil over medium-high heat, then reduce the heat and simmer gently for 1 hour or until the chicken is falling away from the bones.

Add the remaining vegetables to the pan and simmer for another 6–8 minutes or until the vegetables are cooked.

Turn off the heat and let rest for 5–10 minutes. Remove the skin from the chicken, if desired, then divide the chicken among 4 deep serving bowls with the vegetables. Serve with spoonfuls of the broth ladled over.

mango & smoked chicken salad

Calories per serving **378**
Serves **4**
Preparation time **15 minutes**

2 ripe **avocados**, halved,
  pitted and peeled
2 tablespoons **lemon juice**
1 small **mango**
handful of **watercress**
¼ cup finely sliced cooked
  beets
6 oz **smoked chicken**

Dressing
3 tablespoons **olive oil**
1 teaspoon **whole-grain
  mustard**
1 teaspoon **honey**
2 teaspoons **cider vinegar**
salt and **pepper**

Slice or dice the avocado flesh and put it in a shallow bowl with the lemon juice.

Cut the mango in half on either side of the central pit, peel away the skin and slice or dice the flesh.

Make the dressing. Whisk together the oil, mustard, honey, and vinegar. Season to taste with salt and pepper. Remove the avocado from the lemon juice and mix the juice into the dressing.

Arrange the watercress and beets on 4 plates or in a salad bowl and add the avocado and mango. Drizzle the dressing over the salad and stir to combine. Thinly slice the chicken and top the salad with the meat. Serve immediately.

For smoked chicken, white bean, & thyme salad, rinse and drain 2 (15 oz) cans cannellini beans and mix with 1 cup halved cherry tomatoes, 2½ cups arugula, ⅓ cup pitted green olives, and 1 tablespoon chopped thyme. Make the dressing by whisking 1 teaspoon Dijon mustard, 2 tablespoons cider vinegar, ¼ cup olive oil, and 1 tablespoon chopped thyme. Dress the salad and serve with 6 oz thinly sliced smoked chicken. **Calories per serving 347**

chicken couscous salad

Calories per serving **378**
Serves **4**
Preparation time **20 minutes,**
 plus marinating
Cooking time **20 minutes**

4 boneless, skinless **chicken
 breasts**, each about 4 oz
1 cup **couscous**
¾ cup hot **chicken stock**
1 **pomegranate**
zest and juice of 1 **orange**
small bunch of **fresh cilantro**
small bunch of **mint**

Marinade
1 ½ tablespoons **curry paste**
 (tikka masala)
5 tablespoons **plain yogurt**
1 teaspoon **olive oil**
2 tablespoons **lemon juice**

Make a marinade by mixing the curry paste, yogurt, and oil. Put the chicken in a nonmetallic dish, cover with half the marinade, and let stand for at least 1 hour.

Put the couscous in a bowl, add the hot stock, cover and let stand for 8 minutes.

Meanwhile, cut the pomegranate in half and remove the seeds. When the couscous is done, add them to the couscous with the orange zest and juice.

Remove the chicken from the marinade, reserving the marinade, and transfer to a foil-lined baking sheet. Cook in a preheated oven, 375°F, for 6–7 minutes, then transfer to a preheated hot broiler and cook for 2 minutes until caramelized. Cover with foil and let rest for 5 minutes.

Coarsely chop the cilantro and mint, reserving some whole cilantro for garnish, and add to the couscous. Thinly slice the chicken. Spoon the couscous onto plates and add the chicken. Thin the reserved marinade with the lemon juice and drizzle over the couscous. Garnish with the reserved cilantro and serve immediately.

For pomegranate vinaigrette, an alternative dressing for this salad, whisk together ⅔ cup pomegranate juice, 2 tablespoons pomegranate molasses (available from Middle Eastern stores and some supermarkets), 2 tablespoons red wine vinegar, and 3 tablespoons olive oil. **Calories per serving 468**

sherried chicken stroganoff

Calories per serving **379**
  (excluding rice)
Serves **4**
Preparation time **10 minutes**
Cooking time **about**
  10 minutes

2 tablespoons **butter**
2 tablespoons **sunflower oil**
4 boneless, skinless **chicken
  breasts** about 5 oz each, cut
  into long, thin slices
2 **onions**, thinly sliced
1 teaspoon **paprika**
2 teaspoons **mild mustard**
6 tablespoons **dry** or **medium
  dry sherry**
6 tablespoons **water**
6 tablespoons **sour cream**
salt and **pepper**

To serve (optional)
boiled rice

Heat the butter and oil in a large skillet, add the
chicken and onions and fry over medium heat, stirring,
for 6–7 minutes or until the chicken and onions are a
deep golden color.

Stir in the paprika, then add the mustard, sherry,
measured water, and salt and pepper.

Cook for 2–3 minutes or until the chicken is cooked
through, then add the cream and swirl together. Spoon
onto plates and serve with rice, if desired.

For chicken & fennel stroganoff, fry the sliced
chicken breasts in the butter and oil as above, replacing
one of the onions with 1 small, thinly sliced fennel bulb.
When golden add the mustard (omit the paprika) and
6 tablespoons Pernod, instead of the sherry, flaming
it with a taper. Add the measured water and salt and
pepper as above. Cook for 2–3 minutes or until the
chicken is cooked through, then add 6 tablespoons
half-fat crème fraîche and stir until just melted. Serve
as above. **Calories per serving 427**

indonesian yellow drumstick curry

Calories per serving **383**
Serves **4**
Preparation time **15 minutes**
Cooking time **40–45 minutes**

2 **red chiles**, coarsely
    chopped, plus extra to garnish
2 **shallots**, coarsely chopped
3 **garlic cloves**, chopped
¼ cup chopped **lemon grass**
    (outer leaves removed)
1 tablespoon peeled and finely
    chopped **galangal**
2 teaspoons **ground turmeric**
1 teaspoon **cayenne pepper**
1 teaspoon **ground cilantro**
1 teaspoon **ground cumin**
¼ teaspoon **ground cinnamon**
3 tablespoons **Thai fish sauce**
1 tablespoon **palm sugar** or
    brown sugar
4 **kaffir lime leaves**, shredded
1¾ cups **reduced-fat
    coconut milk**
juice of ½ **lime**
8 large **chicken drumsticks**,
    skinned
7 oz **baby new potatoes**,
    peeled
10–12 **Thai basil leaves**, to
    garnish

Place the chiles, shallots, garlic, lemon grass, galangal, turmeric, cayenne, cilantro, cumin, cinnamon, fish sauce, sugar, lime leaves, coconut milk, and lime juice in a food processor, and blend until fairly smooth.

Arrange the chicken drumsticks in a single layer in an ovenproof casserole. Add the potatoes. Pour over the spice paste to coat the chicken and potatoes evenly. Cover and cook in a preheated oven, 350°F, for 40–45 minutes, until the chicken is cooked through and the potatoes are tender. Serve hot, garnished with basil and chopped red chile.

For tandoori drumstick curry, arrange 8 large, skinned chicken drumsticks in a single layer in an ovenproof casserole. Mix 1¼ cups fat-free plain yogurt with ¼ cup tandoori paste and the juice of 2 lemons. Season and pour this mixture over the chicken to coat evenly. Cover and cook in a preheated oven, 350°F, for 35–40 minutes, then uncover and continue to cook for 10–15 minutes or until cooked through. Serve warm with a crisp green salad. **Calories per serving 360**

barbecued chicken with apple slaw

Calories per serving **384**
Serves **4**
Preparation time **25 minutes**
Cooking time **15 minutes**

6 tablespoons **ketchup**
2 tablespoons **Worcestershire sauce**
2 tablespoons **red wine vinegar**
2 tablespoons packed **light brown sugar**
2 teaspoons **English mustard**
12 **chicken wings**

For the apple slaw
1 **dessert apple**, cored, diced
1 tablespoon **lemon juice**
1 **carrot**, coarsely grated
3 **scallions**, thinly sliced
2 cups finely shredded **white cabbage**, core discarded
6 tablespoons **reduced-fat mayonnaise**
salt and **pepper**

Mix the ketchup, Worcestershire sauce, vinegar, sugar, and mustard together. Put the chicken on a foil-lined baking sheet or broiler rack, then brush with the ketchup mixture.

Cook the chicken wings under a preheated broiler or on a barbecue for about 15 minutes, turning once or twice, until a deep brown and the chicken is cooked through.

Meanwhile, mix all the slaw ingredients together in a bowl, then spoon into a bowl. Put the chicken wings onto a plate and serve with plenty of paper napkins for sticky fingers.

For Chinese barbecued chicken wings, mix ¼ cup hoisin sauce with ¼ cup orange juice, 2 tablespoons Chinese rice wine or dry sherry, and 2 tablespoons ketchup. Brush over the chicken and grill or barbecue as above. **Calories per serving 376**

warm chicken ciabatta with salsa

Calories per serving **384**
Serves **4**
Preparation time **15 minutes**
Cooking time **15–20 minutes**

1 tablespoon **olive oil**
2 **chicken breasts**, each about
   5 oz, sliced lengthwise
pepper
1 **ciabatta loaf**, halved
2 **ripe tomatoes**, coarsely
   chopped
1 small **red onion**, thinly sliced
3 tablespoons chopped
   parsley
arugula, to serve
reduced-fat mayonnaise, to
   taste
mustard, to taste

Heat the oil in a large, heavy-based skillet. Toss the chicken breasts with plenty of pepper, add to the pan and cook, turning occasionally, over high heat for 15 minutes or until golden and cooked through.

Cut the ciabatta loaf halves into 4 pieces and cook them, cut side down, on a preheated hot ridged grill pan for 1–2 minutes or until lightly toasted.

Mix together the chopped tomatoes, onion, and parsley to make a salsa.

Arrange the slices of chicken on the 4 ciabatta bases and top with salsa and arugula leaves. Spread the ciabatta tops with mayonnaise and mustard, place on top and serve.

For hot tomato, caramelized onion, & chicken open sandwich, heat 2 tablespoons olive oil and cook 1 finely sliced red onion over moderate heat, for 15 minutes or until soft and caramelized. Add 1 tablespoon brown sugar for the final 1 minute of cooking, then set aside. Make a salsa by mixing 1 finely chopped tomato with 3 tablespoons chopped cilantro, season and set aside. Heat 1 tablespoon olive oil and cook 2 thinly sliced chicken breasts for 4–5 minutes or until golden. Slice 1 ciabatta loaf in half and spread with reduced-fat mayonnaise. Top with the hot chicken, onion, and salsa. Add arugula leaves and serve. **Calories per serving 444**

chicken with pimento pureé

Calories per serving **385**
Serves **8**
Preparation time **15 minutes,**
plus cooling
Cooking time **1¾–2¼ hours**

1 **whole chicken**, about 4 lb
1 **onion**, quartered
1 **carrot**, sliced
2 **celery sticks**, sliced
4 **juniper berries**, crushed
1 **bay leaf**
4–6 stalks **parsley**
6 **peppercorns**, lightly crushed
parsley, chopped, to garnish
zucchini slices, griddled, to
serve (optional)
salt

For the pimento pureé
8 oz canned **pimentos**,
drained, rinsed, chopped
1 tablespoon **tomato paste**
2 tablespoons **mango
chutney**
7 fl oz **low-fat plain yogurt**
salt and **pepper**

Put the chicken, onion, carrot, celery, juniper berries,
bay leaf, parsley, peppercorns, and salt into a saucepan.
Cover with water. Bring to a boil, cover the saucepan,
and simmer for 1½–2 hours or until the chicken is
cooked when tested. Let the chicken cool in the stock.
Lift out the chicken, drain and dry it. Reserve the stock,
discarding the bay leaf. Skin the chicken and slice the
meat from the bones.

To make the puree, put the pimentos, 2 tablespoons of
the reserved chicken stock, tomato paste and chutney
into a saucepan and bring to a boil. Transfer to a
blender or food processor and blend until smooth. Set
aside to cool. Blend the cooled pimento mixture with
the yogurt and season to taste.

Arrange the chicken on a serving dish and pour over
the sauce. Garnish with the parsley and serve with
griddled zucchini, if desired.

For mini chicken meatballs with pimento puree, mix
1 lb ground chicken with 3 chopped scallions, 2 cloves
of finely chopped garlic, 1 egg yolk, and seasoning.
Shape into 20 small meatballs, chill for 30 minutes, then
fry in 1 tablespoon sunflower oil for 5 minutes. Transfer
to a preheated oven, 375°F, for 15 minutes, until cooked
through. Serve with the sauce as above, rice, and a
tomato and onion salad. **Calories per serving 366**

jerk chicken wings

Calories per serving **387**
Serves **4**
Preparation time **5 minutes,**
  plus marinating
Cooking time **12 minutes**

12 large **chicken wings**
2 tablespoons **olive oil**
1 tablespoon j**erk seasoning
  mix**
juice of ½ **lemon**
1 teaspoon **salt**
chopped **parsley**, to garnish
lemon wedges, to serve

Put the chicken wings in a nonmetallic dish. Whisk together the oil, jerk seasoning mix, lemon juice, and salt in a small bowl, pour over the wings, and stir well until evenly coated. Cover and let marinate in the refrigerator for at least 30 minutes or overnight.

Arrange the chicken wings on a broiler rack and cook under a preheated broiler, basting halfway through cooking with any remaining marinade, for 6 minutes on each side or until cooked through, tender, and lightly charred at the edges. Increase or reduce the temperature setting of the broiler, if necessary, to make sure that the wings cook through.

Sprinkle with the chopped parsley and serve immediately with lemon wedges for squeezing over.

For sweet potato mash, to serve, peel 1 ½ lb sweet potatoes and cut them into chunks. Steam or boil until tender, then mash with 2 tablespoons sour cream and a good grinding of nutmeg. Season with salt and pepper. **Calories per serving 194**

balti chicken

Calories per serving **388**
Serves **4**
Preparation time **15 minutes**
Cooking time **20–25 minutes**

1 tablespoon **peanut oil**
2 **onions**, thinly sliced
2 **fresh red chiles**, seeded
 and thinly sliced
6–8 **curry leaves**
¾ cup **water**
3 **garlic cloves**, crushed
1 teaspoon peeled and finely
 grated **fresh ginger root**
1 tablespoon **ground cilantro**
2 tablespoons **Madras curry**
 powder
1 lb **ground chicken**
2½ cups **fresh** or **frozen peas**
¼ cup **lemon juice**
small handful of chopped
 mint leaves
small handful of chopped
 fresh cilantro
salt

To serve
chapatis (1 per person)
fat-free plain yogurt (2
 tablespoons per serving)

Heat the oil in a large wok or skillet over medium heat. Add the onion, chile and curry leaves, and stir-fry for 4–5 minutes. Add ¼ cup of the measured water and continue to stir-fry for another 2–3 minutes.

Add the garlic, ginger, ground cilantro, curry powder, and chicken, and stir-fry over high heat for 10 minutes. Add the remaining measured water and the peas, and continue to cook for 6–8 minutes, until the chicken is cooked through.

Remove from the heat and stir in the lemon juice and herbs. Season to taste, and serve immediately with warmed chapatis and yogurt.

For creamy chicken & vegetable curry, heat 1 tablespoon peanut oil in a large wok or skillet. Add 1 chopped onion, 1 sliced red chile, 6 curry leaves, 2 teaspoons each of crushed fresh ginger root and garlic, and 2 tablespoons mild curry powder. Stir-fry for 1–2 minutes, then add 1¼ lb diced boneless, skinless chicken breasts. Stir-fry for 3–4 minutes, then add 2 cups chicken stock and ¾ cup reduced-fat coconut milk. Bring to a boil and cook for 12–15 minutes or until the chicken is cooked through. Stir in 1¼ cups frozen peas and cook over high heat for 4–5 minutes. Season and serve with rice (approximately 3 tablespoons per person). **Calories per serving 470**

lemony poached chicken

Calories per serving **389**
Serves **4**
Preparation time **10 minutes**
Cooking time **1¾–2 hours**

1 **whole chicken**, about
   3–4 lb
3 **shallots**, halved
2 **garlic cloves**, lightly crushed
1 **celery stick**, coarsely
   chopped
1 **rosemary sprig**
8 black **peppercorns**
½ cup **balsamic vinegar**
1 **preserved lemon**, chopped
1 small bunch of **sage**, leaves
   removed
2 tablespoons **extra virgin**
   canola oil
salt and **pepper**
steamed vegetables such
   as **asparagus** and **broccoli**,
   to serve

Put the chicken, shallots, garlic, celery, rosemary, and black peppercorns in a large saucepan. Add the balsamic vinegar and pour in enough cold water to almost cover the chicken. Place over medium heat and bring slowly to a boil, skimming the surface to remove any scummy froth. Cover and simmer gently for 1 hour.

Add the preserved lemon and half the sage leaves, then simmer gently for another 15–30 minutes, until the juices run clear when the thickest part of the chicken leg is pierced with a knife. Remove from the pan and place in a deep dish, cover with foil, and let rest. Increase the heat and boil the stock for 20–25 minutes or until reduced by half. Remove from the heat and let cool slightly. Season to taste.

Heat the oil in a small skillet and pan-fry the remaining sage leaves for 30 seconds until crisp. Remove with a slotted spoon and drain on paper towels.

Cut the chicken meat from the carcass, discarding the skin, and spoon into shallow bowls with plenty of cooking broth. Garnish with the crisp sage leaves and serve with steamed asparagus and broccoli.

For lemony chicken breasts, replace the whole chicken with 4 large boneless, skinless chicken breasts. Place in a large saucepan with the garlic, rosemary, peppercorns, balsamic vinegar, and preserved lemon and just cover with water. Simmer gently for about 12 minutes or until the chicken is cooked through. Cut the chicken into thick slices and serve in bowls with the chicken broth, garnished with sage leaves as above.
Calories per serving 276

grilled chicken baguettes

Calories per serving **391**
Serves **4**
Preparation time **10 minutes**
Cooking time **8–10 minutes**

4 small **part-baked
wholegrain** or **seeded
baguettes**
2 large boneless, skinless
chicken breasts, about
10 oz in total
1 teaspoon **olive oil**
¼ cup **roasted red pepper
pesto**
2 tablespoons **sunflower
seeds**
handful of **arugula leaves**
salt and **pepper**

Salad
¼ **cucumber**, halved, seeded,
and thinly sliced
2 tablespoons chopped **mint**
1 tablespoon **lemon juice**

Place the baguettes on a baking sheet and bake
in a preheated oven, 400°F, for 8–10 minutes, or
according to the package instructions, until crisp.

Meanwhile, lay a chicken breast between 2 sheets
of plastic wrap and flatten with a rolling pin or meat
mallet. Repeat with the remaining chicken breast. Heat
a ridged grill pan over medium-high heat until hot. Rub
the oil over the chicken breasts, season with salt and
pepper, and cook on the hot grill pan for 2–3 minutes
or until slightly charred. Turn the chicken breasts over
and cook for another 2–3 minutes or until slightly
charred and cooked through but not dry. Remove from
the pan, cover with foil, and let rest.

Make the salad. Mix together the cucumber, mint,
lemon juice, and a little salt and pepper in a small bowl.

Slice the chicken into thick slices. Cut the baguettes in
half lengthwise, spread with the red pepper pesto, then
fill with the chicken and the cucumber salad. Sprinkle
with sunflower seeds and add a few arugula leaves. Cut
in half and serve immediately.

For grilled chicken & spicy couscous, prepare
and cook 4 chicken breasts as above and cut into
thick slices. Meanwhile, cook 1⅔ cups whole-wheat
couscous according to the package instructions, then
fork through 2 tablespoons homemade (see page
192) or store-bought harissa. Serve the chicken on the
couscous with the cucumber salad as above. **Calories
per serving 457**

under 500 calories

thai chicken satay

Calories per serving **497**
Serves **4**
Preparation time **30 minutes,**
   plus marinating
Cooking time **16 minutes**

4 boneless, skinless **chicken
   breasts**, cut into thin slices
3 **garlic cloves**, finely chopped
2½ inch piece **ginger root**,
   peeled and grated
2 tablespoons **light soy sauce**
2 tablespoons **lemon juice**
1 tablespoon **sunflower oil**
2 **shallots** or ½ **onion**, finely
   sliced
1 small hot **Thai chile**, thinly
   sliced
¼ cup **crunchy peanut butter**
¾ cup canned **low-fat
   coconut milk**
2 teaspoons **fish sauce**
1 tablespoon **light soy sauce**

To serve
boiled rice (approximately 2
   tablespoons per serving)
green salad (optional)

Mix the chicken with 2 of the garlic cloves, a third of
the ginger, the light soy sauce and lemon juice and then
let stand for 30 minutes.

Heat the sunflower oil in a small saucepan. Add the
shallots or onion and fry gently until softened but not
brown. Mix in the remaining garlic and ginger and
the chile, and cook for 1 minute before adding all the
remaining ingredients. Simmer gently for 5 minutes.

Thread the marinaded chicken slices in a zigzag pattern
onto 12 thin metal skewers. Cook under a hot broiler for
10 minutes, turning once or twice until the chicken is
browned and cooked through. Garnish with lime wedges
and serve with rice (about 2 tablespoons per person).

grilled tandoori chicken

Calories per serving **401**

Serves **4**

Preparation time **10 minutes,**
  plus marinating

Cooking time **16–20 minutes**

4 x 4 oz boneless, skinless
  chicken breasts

¼ cup **tandoori paste** or
  powder

¼ cup **olive oil**

2 **red onions**, finely sliced

4 **tomatoes**, finely sliced

bunch of **fresh cilantro,**
  coarsely chopped

¼ cup **lemon juice**

lemon wedges, grilled
  (optional), to serve

salt and **pepper**

Using a sharp knife, make a series of small slashes in the flesh of the chicken breasts and rub in the tandoori paste or powder. Let marinate in the refrigerator overnight.

Heat 1 tablespoon olive oil in a ridged grill pan (or an ordinary skillet). Cook the marinated chicken breasts for 8–10 minutes on each side, allowing the authentic tandoori charred color to appear, or until cooked throroughly.

Mix the red onions, tomatoes, and cilantro together with the lemon juice, remaining olive oil, and seasoning in a small bowl. Serve the salad with the tandoori chicken, accompanied by lemon wedges, grilled if desired.

For griddled harissa chicken, rub the slashed chicken with 4 teaspoons harissa paste (see page 192) instead of the tandoori paste or powder. Marinate, then fry. Soak 1 cup couscous in 1¾ cups boiling water for 5 minutes. Stir in 2 tablespoons olive oil, 3 tablespoons fresh chopped cilantro, and seasoning. Serve with lemon wedges. **Calories per serving 422**

chicken tacos

Calories per serving **403**
Serves **4**
Preparation time **5 minutes**
Cooking time **20 minutes**

1 tablespoon **vegetable oil**
1 lb **ground chicken**
2 **garlic cloves**, crushed
1 (1¼ oz) package **taco** or
   fajita seasoning mix
juice of 1 **lime**
8 **taco shells**

To serve
¼ cup **tomato salsa**
¼ cup **fat-free Greek yogurt**
   (1 tablespoon per person)
crisp lettuce, shredded
1 cup shredded **reduced-fat
   cheddar cheese** (¼ cup per
   person)
lime wedges

Heat the oil in a skillet, add the ground chicken and stir-fry, keeping the meat in clumps. Add the garlic and seasoning mix and continue cooking for 15 minutes, adding a little water if the mixture becomes too dry. Stir in the lime juice.

Warm the taco shells according to the instructions on the package. Spoon in the chicken mixture and top with tomato salsa, yogurt, shredded lettuce and cheese, with lime wedges on the side.

For Tex–Mex chicken & beans, fry 1 lb ground chicken in 1 tablespoon sunflower oil over a high heat with 1¼ oz taco or fajita seasoning mix for 15 minutes until clumpy and cooked. Add 1 cup tomato puree or sauce and 7½ oz can kidney beans, rinsed and drained. Heat through and serve on thick slices of toast (1 per person) from a crusty loaf. **Calories per serving 328**

thai chicken noodle salad

Calories per serving **404**
Serves **4**
Preparation time **10 minutes**
Cooking time **10 minutes**

8 oz **thin rice noodles**
6 tablespoons **Thai sweet
  chili sauce**
2 tablespoons **Thai fish sauce**
juice of 2 **limes**
2 cooked boneless, skinless
  chicken breasts
1 **cucumber**, cut into ribbons
1 **red chile**, finely chopped
small handful of **fresh cilantro**

Put the noodles in a large heatproof bowl and pour boiling water over to cover. Let stand for 6–8 minutes until tender, then drain and rinse well under cold running water.

Whisk together the sweet chili sauce, fish sauce, and lime juice in a bowl. Shred the chicken and toss with the dressing to coat.

Add the noodles, cucumber, and chile to the chicken mixture and toss gently to combine. Sprinkle with the cilantro and serve immediately.

For Mediterranean pasta salad, cook 8 oz fusilli according to package instructions and allow to cool. Meanwhile mix together 3 tablespoons each of balsamic vinegar and olive oil and toss with the chicken as above. Add the cooked pasta, and sprinkle with a small handful of basil leaves instead of cilantro. **Calories per serving 399**

thai barbecued chicken

Calories per serving **406**
Serves **4–6**
Preparation time **20–25 minutes,** plus chilling
Cooking time **30–40 minutes or 10–15 minutes,** depending on type of chicken

3 lb **whole chicken,** spatchcocked, or part-boned **chicken breasts**
2 inch piece **galangal**, peeled, finely chopped
4 **garlic cloves**, crushed
1 large **red chile**, finely chopped
4 **shallots**, finely chopped
2 tablespoons finely chopped **fresh cilantro**
²/₃ cup **thick coconut milk**
chive flowers, to garnish
salt and **pepper**

To serve
lime wedges

Rub the chicken all over with salt and pepper and place in a shallow container.

Put the galangal, garlic, red chili, shallots, and cilantro in a food processor and blend to a paste, or use a mortar and pestle. Add the coconut milk and mix until well blended. Pour over the chicken, cover, and let marinate overnight in the refrigerator.

Remove the chicken from the marinade, place it on a hot barbecue and cook for 30–40 minutes for spatchcocked chicken and 10–15 minutes for chicken breasts, turning and basting regularly with the remaining marinade. The whole chicken is cooked when the tip of a sharp knife inserted in one of the legs reveals clear juices.

Let the chicken stand for 5 minutes, then chop it into small pieces with a cleaver. Garnish with chive flowers and eat with fingers. Serve with the sweet chili sauce as well as lime wedges.

For sweet chili sauce, to serve as an accompaniment, wear a pair of plastic gloves and remove the seeds from 15 medium red chiles then finely chop the flesh. Place the chiles in a saucepan with 1¼ cups granulated sugar, ²/₃ cup rice wine vinegar, and ²/₃ cup water. Heat gently to dissolve the sugar, then increase the heat and simmer briskly for 20–25 minutes or until the liquid has reduced to a syrup. Pour the sauce into a sterilized glass jar or bottle and keep in the refrigerator until required.
Calories per serving 92

chicken & adzuki bean salad

Calories per serving **408**
Serves **4**
Preparation time **15 minutes**
Cooking time **2–3 minutes**

1 **green bell pepper**, cored,
  seeded, and chopped
1 **red bell pepper**, cored,
  seeded, and chopped
1 small **red onion**, finely
  chopped
1 (15 oz) can **adzuki beans**,
  drained
1 (8 oz) can **corn kernals**,
  drained
small bunch of **fresh cilantro**,
  chopped
1 cup unsweetened **coconut
  chips** or **flakes**
8 oz cooked **chicken breast**,
  shredded
small handful of **alfalfa shoots**
  (optional)

Dressing
3 tablespoons **light peanut oil**
2 tablespoons **light soy sauce**
2 teaspoons peeled and
  grated **fresh ginger root**
1 tablespoon **rice vinegar**

Mix together the green and red peppers, onion, adzuki beans, corn, and half the cilantro in a large bowl. Whisk together the dressing ingredients in a separate bowl, then stir 3 tablespoons into the bean salad. Spoon the salad into serving dishes.

Place the coconut chips or flakes in a nonstick skillet over medium heat and dry-fry for 2–3 minutes or until lightly golden brown, stirring continuously.

Arrange the shredded chicken and remaining cilantro over the bean salad and sprinkle with the toasted coconut and alfalfa shoots, if using. Serve with the remaining dressing.

For chicken, avocado, & coconut salad, dice the flesh of 1 firm, ripe avocado, toss in 1 tablespoon of lime juice, and add to the bean salad. Serve as above.
Calories per serving 496

herby quinoa with lemon

Calories per serving **409**
Serves **4**
Preparation time **15 minutes**
Cooking time **15 minutes**

1 cup **quinoa**
1 tablespoon **olive oil**
1 **onion**, chopped
1 **garlic clove**, crushed
4 boneless, skinless **chicken breasts**, sliced
1 teaspoon **ground cilantro**
½ teaspoon **ground cumin**
½ cup **dried cranberries**
½ cup **no-need-to-soak dried apricots**, chopped
¼ cup chopped **parsley**
¼ cup chopped **mint**
finely grated zest of **1 lemon**
salt and **pepper**

Cook the quinoa in a pan of lightly salted boiling water for 15 minutes until tender, then drain.

Meanwhile, heat the oil in a large skillet, add the onion and cook, stirring, for 5 minutes to soften. Add the garlic, chicken, cilantro, and cumin and cook for another 8–10 minutes, until the chicken is cooked.

Season the quinoa with salt and pepper. Add the chicken mixture, cranberries, apricots, herbs, and lemon zest. Stir well and serve warm or cold.

For chicken & apricot moroccan couscous, put ½ cup Moroccan-flavored couscous in a bowl, cover with boiling water, cover the bowl with plastic wrap and let stand for 8 minutes. When all the water has been absorbed, stir in 8 oz chopped cooked chicken, ¾ cup no-need-to-soak apricots, and 1 (7½ oz) can chickpeas, rinsed and drained. **Calories per serving 384**

thai chicken shells with cilantro

Calories per serving **410**
Serves **4**
Preparation time **10 minutes**
Cooking time **15 minutes**

1 teaspoon **vegetable oil**
2 **chicken breasts**, about
   5 oz each, sliced
1 tablespoon red or green
   Thai curry paste
1¾ cups **coconut milk**
1¼ cups **basmati rice**
3 tablespoons chopped **fresh
   cilantro**
3 **scallions**, sliced
4 small **crisphead lettuces**,
   separated into individual
   leaves
2 **limes**, cut into wedges

Heat the oil in a nonstick skillet, add the chicken, and fry for 2 minutes.

Add the curry paste and continue to fry for 1 minute, then add half the coconut milk, bring to a boil, and simmer gently for 10 minutes.

Meanwhile, put the rice in a saucepan with the remaining coconut milk and ½ cup water. Bring to a boil, then reduce the heat, cover, and simmer for 10–12 minutes, until the liquid is absorbed, adding a little extra water if necessary. Turn the heat off and stir in the cilantro.

Put chicken and scallion slices and some rice on a lettuce leaf and squeeze the lime wedges over the filled shells before eating.

For quick Chinese-style stir-fry, cook 10 oz chicken strips for 1 minute in 3 tablespoons vegetable oil with 2 teaspoons chopped garlic. Add 1 cup sliced green bell pepper and 5 seeded and sliced red chiles and cook for a minute, then stir in ⅓ cup sliced onion, 1 tablespoon oyster sauce, 1 teaspoon fish sauce, ½ tablespoon light soy sauce, and ¼ teaspoon dark soy sauce. Stir-fry until the chicken is cooked through then serve. **Calories per serving 200**

fast chicken curry

Calories per serving **413**
Serves **4**
Preparation time **5 minutes**
Cooking time **20–25 minutes**

3 tablespoons **olive oil**
1 **onion**, finely chopped
¼ cup **medium curry paste**
8 boneless, skinless **chicken
    thighs**, cut into thin strips
1 (14½ oz) can **diced
    tomatoes**
8 oz **broccoli**, broken into
    small florets, stalks peeled
    and sliced
½ cup **reduced-fat coconut
    milk**
salt and **pepper**

Heat the oil in a deep nonstick saucepan over medium heat. Add the onion and cook for 3 minutes, until soft and translucent. Add the curry paste and cook, stirring, for 1 minute, until fragrant.

Add the chicken, tomatoes, broccoli, and coconut milk to the pan. Bring to a boil, then reduce the heat, cover, and simmer gently over low heat for 15–20 minutes until the chicken is cooked through.

Remove from the heat, season well with salt and pepper and serve immediately.

For chicken patties with curry sauce, follow the first stage of the recipe above, then add the tomatoes, 4 cups young spinach leaves, and the reduced-fat coconut milk (omitting the chicken and broccoli), and cook as directed. Meanwhile, finely chop 1 lb cooked chicken breasts. Transfer to a bowl and add 4 finely chopped scallions, 2 tablespoons chopped fresh cilantro, 1 cup fresh white bread crumbs, a squeeze of lemon juice, and 1 beaten egg. Season with salt and pepper. Mix well, then form into 16 patties. Roll in ½ cup fresh white bread crumbs to coat. Brush vegetable oil around a large skillet over medium heat. Add the patties, cooking in batches, and pan-fry on each side until golden brown and cooked through. Serve hot with the curry sauce. **Calories per serving 490**

burmese chicken noodle curry

Calories per serving **403**
Serves **6**
Preparation time **20 minutes**
Cooking time **about 1 hour**

2 lb boneless, skinless
   chicken thighs, cut into
   bite-size pieces
2 **onions**, chopped
5 **garlic cloves**, chopped
1 teaspoon finely grated **fresh
   ginger root**
2 tablespoons **sunflower oil**
½ teaspoon **Burmese shrimp
   paste** (belacan)
1¾ cups **coconut milk**
1 tablespoon **medium curry
   powder**
10½ oz **dried rice vermicelli**
salt and **pepper**

To garnish
chopped **fresh cilantro**
finely chopped **red onion**
fried **garlic slivers**
sliced **red chiles**
lime wedges

Season the chicken pieces and set aside. Process the onion, garlic, and ginger in a food processor until smooth. If necessary, add a little water to assist in blending the mixture. Heat the oil in a large pan. Add the onion mixture and shrimp paste and cook, stirring, over high heat for about 5 minutes.

Add the chicken and cook over medium heat, turning it until it browns.

Pour in the coconut milk and add the curry powder. Bring to a boil, reduce the heat and simmer, covered, for about 30 minutes, stirring from time to time. Uncover the pan and cook for another 15 minutes or until the chicken is tender and cooked through.

Place the noodles in a bowl, cover with boiling water and set aside for 10 minutes. Drain the noodles and divide them among 4 large warm serving bowls. Ladle over the curry, and garnish with chopped cilantro, chopped red onion, fried garlic slivers, sliced red chiles, and lime wedges.

For tofu noodle curry, replace the chicken with 14½ oz cubed tofu, then add ½ cup each of baby corn and snowpeas to the curry 5 minutes before the end of cooking. Finish as above. **Calories per serving 313**

yogurt chicken with greek salad

Calories per serving **420**
Serves **4**
Preparation time **10 minutes**
Cooking time **10 minutes**

²/₃ cup **fat-free Greek yogurt**
1 **garlic clove**, crushed
2 tablespoons **olive oil**
finely grated zest and juice of
   1 **lemon**
1 teaspoon **ground cumin**
4 boneless, skinless **chicken
   breasts**, cut into bite-size
   chunks
1¹/₃ cups chopped **cucumber**
1 **red onion**, sliced
4 **tomatoes**, cut into slim
   wedges
16 **black ripe olives**
6 oz **feta cheese**, crumbled
1 small **romaine lettuce**, torn

For the dressing
1 tablespoon **lemon juice**
2 tablespoons **olive oil**
1 tablespoon chopped **fresh
   oregano** or ½ teaspoon
   dried oregano

Soak 8 small wooden skewers in water and preheat the broiler to high. In a bowl, mix together the yogurt, garlic, olive oil, lemon zest and juice, and cumin. Add the chicken, stir well and then thread onto 8 skewers. Place on a foil-lined broiler pan.

Cook under a preheated hot broiler for 10 minutes, turning occasionally, or until the chicken is cooked and beginning to char in places.

Meanwhile, in a salad bowl mix together the cucumber, onion, tomatoes, olives, feta, and lettuce.

Make the dressing by whisking together the lemon juice, oil, and fresh or dried oregano. Pour the dressing over the salad and lightly mix together. Serve with the chicken skewers.

For yogurt chicken & bulgar wheat salad, prepare the chicken skewers as above. While they are cooking put ½ cup bulgur wheat in a pan with 1¾ cups boiling water. Cover and simmer for 15 minutes, until the liquid has been absorbed. Cool slightly before mixing with chopped cucumber, 1 sliced red onion, 4 chopped tomatoes, 16 black olives, 6 oz crumbled feta cheese, and 2 tablespoons each of chopped parsley and chopped mint. **Calories per serving 414**

quinoa salad with seared chicken

Calories per serving **421**
Serves **4**
Preparation time **25 minutes**
Cooking time **22 minutes**

1 cup **quinoa**
¼ **cucumber**, finely diced
1 small **green bell pepper**,
   cored, seeded, and finely
   diced
6 **scallions**, trimmed, thinly
   sliced
¾ cup **frozen peas**, just
   defrosted
grated zest and juice of
   1 **lemon**
1 tablespoon **olive oil**
1 tablespoon **harissa paste**
4 boneless, skinless **chicken
   breasts**, cut into long
   thin slices
small bunch **mint**, finely
   chopped

For the dressing
2 tablespoons **olive oil**
1 tablespoon **harissa paste**
grated zest and juice of
   1 **lemon**
salt

Add the quinoa to a saucepan of boiling water and simmer for about 10 minutes or according to package instructions until just tender, then drain in a fine sieve.

Make the dressing by mixing the olive oil, harissa, lemon zest and juice, and a little salt in a salad bowl. Stir in the hot quinoa and let cool, then mix in the cucumber, bell pepper, scallions and frozen peas.

Mix the lemon zest and juice, oil, and harissa in a shallow bowl, then add the chicken and toss well. Heat a ridged grill pan (or ordinary skillet) and cook the chicken in batches for about 6 minutes, turning until browned on both sides and cooked through.

Stir the mint through the quinoa salad, then top with the warm chicken. Serve warm or cold. Any leftovers can be chilled and packed into lunchboxes the following day.

For hot feta & almond quinoa with seared chicken, toss the just-cooked quinoa in the dressing as above. Omit the cucumber, adding 1 seeded and chopped red bell pepper instead, and ⅓ cup golden raisins and ½ cup diced, ready-to-eat dried apricots in place of the peas. Sprinkle with 4 oz drained and crumbled feta cheese and ½ cup toasted sliced almonds. Top with the chicken and serve hot with extra spoonfuls of harissa.
Calories per serving 499

noodles & seven-spice chicken

Calories per serving **437**
Serves **4**
Preparation time **15 minutes**
Cooking time **12 minutes**

3 pieces of **stem ginger** from
  a jar, plus 3 tablespoons of
  the syrup
2 tablespoons **rice wine
  vinegar**
3 tablespoons **light soy sauce**
4 skinned and boned **chicken
  breasts**, about 5–6 oz each
1 tablespoon **Thai seven-
  spice seasoning**
3 tablespoons **stir-fry** or **wok
  oil**
3 **shallots**, thinly sliced
1 cup **baby corn**, halved
10 oz **straight-to-wok
  medium** or **thread noodles**
6 cups **baby spinach**
2 cups **bean sprouts**

Finely shred the pieces of stem ginger. Mix the ginger syrup with the vinegar and soy sauce and reserve.

Halve each chicken breast horizontally and then cut widthwise into thin strips. Toss with the seven-spice seasoning.

Heat the oil in a large skillet or wok and stir-fry the chicken pieces over gentle heat for 5 minutes, until beginning to brown.

Add the shallots and fry for 2 minutes. Stir in the baby corn and fry for 1 minute. Add the noodles and spinach and sprinkle with the shredded stem ginger. Stir-fry, mixing the ingredients together, until the spinach starts to wilt.

Add the bean sprouts and soy sauce mixture and cook, stirring, for another minute or until heated through. Serve immediately.

For chicken with bok choy & shrimp, prepare the ginger syrup, vinegar, and soy sauce as above. Toss 7 oz peeled and deveined raw shrimp with the chicken in seven-spice seasoning and cook as above. Replace the spinach with 4 cups coarsely chopped bok choy.
Calories per serving 459

moroccan chicken & harissa

Calories per serving **438**
  (excluding rice)
Serves **4**
Preparation time **20 minutes**
Cooking time **35 minutes**

1 **onion**, very finely chopped
2 teaspoons **paprika**
1 teaspoon **cumin seeds**
4 x 4 oz boneless, skinless
  chicken breasts
bunch of **fresh cilantro**, finely
  chopped
¼ cup **lemon juice**
3 tablespoons **olive oil**
salt and **pepper**
boiled rice, to serve (optional)

For the harissa
4 **red bell peppers**
4 large **red chiles**
2 **garlic cloves**, crushed
½ teaspoon **cilantro seeds**
1 teaspoon **caraway seeds**
5 tablespoons **olive oil**

Make the harissa by heating a ridged grill pan (or ordinary skillet). Add the whole red peppers and cook for 15 minutes, turning occasionally. The skins will blacken and start to lift. Place the peppers in a plastic bag, seal the bag and set aside for a while (this encourages them to "sweat", making it easier to remove their skins). When cool enough to handle, remove the skin, cores, and seeds from the peppers and place the flesh in a blender or food processor.

Remove the skin, cores, and seeds from the red chiles in the same way. Add the chile flesh to the blender with the garlic, cilantro and caraway seeds, and olive oil. Process to a smooth paste. If not required immediately, place the harissa in a sealable container and pour a thin layer of olive oil over the top. Cover and refrigerate.

Clean the pan and reheat it. Place the onion in a bowl, add the paprika and cumin seeds and mix together. Rub the onion and spice mixture into the chicken breasts. Cook the chicken for 10 minutes on each side, turning once. When cooked, remove from the pan.

Place the cilantro in a bowl and add the lemon juice, olive oil, and a little seasoning. Add the chicken to the bowl and toss well. Serve with the harissa, spinach salad, and rice, if desired.

For a spinach salad, as an accompaniment, rinse and tear 12 oz spinach and add to a pan with any residual water. Cover and cook for 1–2 minutes, until wilted. Stir in 1 clove chopped garlic, ½ cup Greek yogurt, salt, and pepper. Warm and serve. **Calories per serving 50**

chicken fajitas & no-chile salsa

Calories per serving **445**
Serves **4**
Preparation time **20 minutes**
Cooking time **about 5 minutes**

½ teaspoon **ground cilantro**
½ teaspoon **ground cumin**
½ teaspoon **ground paprika**
1 **garlic clove**, crushed
3 tablespoons chopped **fresh cilantro**
12 oz boneless, skinless **chicken breasts**
1 tablespoon **olive oil**
4 **soft flour tortillas**

Salsa

3 ripe **tomatoes**, finely chopped
3 tablespoons chopped **fresh cilantro**
⅛ **cucumber**, finely chopped
1 tablespoon **olive oil**

Guacamole

1 large **avocado**, chopped
grated zest and juice of ½ **lime**

Place all the ground spices, garlic, and cilantro in a mixing bowl. Cut the chicken into bite-size strips and toss in the oil, then add to the spices and toss to coat lightly in the spice mixture.

Make the salsa, mix the tomatoes, cilantro and cucumber in a bowl and drizzle over the oil. Transfer to a serving bowl.

Make the guacamole, mash the avocado with the lime zest and juice and sweet chili sauce, if using, until soft and rough-textured. Transfer to a serving bowl.

Heat a ridged grill pan or heavy skillet and cook the chicken for 3–4 minutes, turning occasionally, until golden and cooked through. Fill the tortillas with the hot chicken slices, guacamole, and salsa, and fold into quarters to serve.

For sour cream chicken tacos, cook the chicken as above and spoon into 8 warmed, store-bought taco shells. Serve 2 per person with ½ tablespoon sour cream and cilantro leaves on each. **Calories per serving 339**

greek-style chicken thighs

Calories per serving **450**
Serves **4**
Preparation time **5 minutes**
Cooking time **30 minutes**

2 tablespoons **olive oil**
4 **chicken thighs**
1 large **red onion**, sliced
1 cup **cherry tomatoes**,
  halved
1 (14½ oz) can **diced
  tomatoes with garlic and
  herbs**
¼ cup **tomato paste**
⅔ cup **kalamata olives**,
  drained
⅔ cup **red wine**
1½ cups trimmed **green
  beans**

To serve
2 oz crumbled **feta cheese**

Heat the oil in large, heavy skillet and cook the chicken thighs and red onion over high heat for 5 minutes, turning once, until golden.

Add the cherry tomatoes and stir-fry for 2 minutes, then add the diced tomatoes and tomato paste and bring to a boil. Reduce the heat, cover, and simmer for 15 minutes. Add the olives, wine, and the beans and stir again. Replace the lid and cook for 5 minutes more until the beans are just tender and the chicken is cooked through.

Serve ladled into warmed bowls and sprinkled with the crumbled feta.

For Greek salad with mixed herb dressing, chop ½ cucumber into chunks and put in a salad bowl with 8 oz sliced cooked chicken, 1 cup halved baby cherry tomatoes, and ⅔ cup kalamata olives. Toss together well. Make a dressing by whisking together ¼ cup olive oil, 2 tablespoons red wine vinegar, 1 teaspoon Dijon mustard, and ½ teaspoon dried mixed herbs. Pour over the salad ingredients and toss well to coat. **Calories per serving 294**

celery, artichoke, & chicken salad

Calories per serving **450**
Serves **4–6**
Preparation time **15 minutes**
Cooking time **5 minutes**

6 thin slices of **rye bread**
2 tablespoons **olive oil**
1 leafy **celery head**
1 cup canned or bottled
  artichoke hearts, drained
  and grilled
2 tablespoons coarsely
  chopped **parsley**
3 **smoked chicken breasts**,
  each about 3½ oz
salt and **pepper**

Dressing
1 teaspoon **Dijon mustard**
2 tablespoons **white wine
  vinegar**
¼ cup **olive oil**

Arrange the rye bread slices on a baking sheet. Drizzle with olive oil, season with salt and pepper, and bake in a preheated oven, 375°F, for 5 minutes, until crispy like croûtons. Remove from the oven and set aside.

Remove the leaves from the celery, reserving all the inside leaves. Finely slice 3 sticks and put them in a large salad bowl with the leaves, add the artichokes and parsley.

Thinly slice the smoked chicken breasts and add to the bowl with the celery and artichokes.

Make the dressing by whisking together the mustard, vinegar, and oil. Drizzle over the salad and lightly mix.

Place a piece of rye toast on each serving plate and top with some salad.

For smoked chicken & cannellini bean salad, rinse and drain 1 (15 oz) can of cannellini beans and put them in a large salad bowl. Add 1 cup sun-blushed tomatoes (oil drained), 1 cup blanched green beans, 1 cup grilled artichokes, and 3 coarsely chopped smoked chicken breasts, each about 3½ oz. In a small bowl whisk 1 tablespoon chopped parsley, 1 tablespoon chopped basil, 1 teaspoon chopped tarragon, 1 crushed garlic clove, 2 tablespoons white wine vinegar, and ¼ cup olive oil. Season with salt and pepper. Toss the dressing through the salad and serve. **Calories per serving 403**

wild rice & grilled chicken salad

Calories per serving **451**
Serves **4**
Preparation time **10 minutes,**
  plus marinating
Cooking time **35 minutes**

1 **garlic clove**, crushed
2 teaspoons **olive oil**
1 teaspoon **balsamic vinegar**
4 small boneless, skinless
  chicken breasts, halved
  horizontally

Rice salad
1 cup mixed **wild** and **basmati
  rice**
2 **red bell peppers**, roasted,
  cored, seeded, and sliced
3 **scallions**, sliced
½ cup **cherry tomatoes**,
  quartered
2 cups **arugula leaves**
3 oz **soft goat cheese**,
  crumbled

Dressing
juice of ½ **lemon**
1 teaspoon **Dijon mustard**
1 teaspoon **honey**
2 tablespoons **olive oil**

Mix together the garlic, olive oil, and vinegar in a non-metallic bowl, add the chicken and coat in the marinade. Cover and let marinate in the refrigerator for at least 30 minutes.

Cook the rice in a saucepan of boiling water according to the package instructions. Drain well and let cool, then mix with the peppers, scallions, tomatoes, arugula, and goat cheese in a large bowl.

Whisk together the dressing ingredients in a bowl and stir into the rice salad. Spoon the salad onto 4 serving plates.

Heat a ridged grill pan until hot and cook the chicken for 3–4 minutes on each side, until cooked through. Immediately before serving, slice the grilled chicken and arrange on top of the salad.

For wild rice, orange, & haloumi salad, make the rice salad as above, replacing the bell peppers with the sliced flesh of 2 oranges and omitting the goat cheese. Make the dressing as above and stir into the salad. Cut 7 oz haloumi cheese into slices, brush with a little olive oil, and season with plenty of black pepper. Heat a ridged grill pan until hot and cook the haloumi for 1–2 minutes on each side, until browned. Arrange on top of the rice salad and serve. **Calories per serving 499**

catalan chicken

Calories per serving **453**
Serves **4**
Preparation time **15 minutes**
Cooking time **25 minutes**

2 tablespoons **olive oil**
½ cup **sliced almonds**
2 **onions**, coarsely chopped
8 **chicken thighs**, boned,
  skinned, and cubed
2 **garlic cloves**, finely chopped
⅔ cup **raisins**
¾ cup **dry sherry**
1 cup **chicken stock** (see
  page 14)
small bunch of **flat-leaf
  parsley**, coarsely chopped
salt and **pepper**

Heat a little of the oil in a large skillet, add the almonds
and fry, stirring for a few minutes until golden. Scoop out
of the pan and set aside.

Add the remaining oil to the pan, then add the onions,
chicken, and garlic and fry over medium heat for 10
minutes, stirring until deep golden. Mix in the raisins,
sherry, stock, and a little salt and pepper.

Simmer for 10 minutes, until the sauce has reduced
slightly and the chicken is cooked through. Sprinkle
with the parsley and serve.

For Normandy chicken, omit the raisins and add
1 cored and diced Granny Smith dessert apple and
2 teaspoons Dijon mustard, replacing the sherry with
¾ cup hard cider. Serve topped with spoonfuls of sour
cream. **Calories per serving 460**

rice noodles with lemon chicken

Calories per serving **458**
Serves **4**
Preparation time **10 minutes**
Cooking time **10 minutes**

4 small boneless **chicken breasts**, skin on
juice of 2 **lemons**
4 tablespoons **sweet chili sauce**
8 oz **dried rice noodles**
small bunch of **flat-leaf parsley**, chopped
small bunch of **cilantro**, chopped
½ **cucumber**, peeled into ribbons with a vegetable peeler
salt and **pepper**
finely chopped **red chile**, to garnish

Mix the chicken with half the lemon juice and the sweet chili sauce in a large bowl and season to taste with salt and pepper.

Lay a chicken breast between 2 sheets of plastic wrap and lightly pound with a mallet to flatten. Repeat with the remaining chicken breasts.

Arrange the chicken on a broiler rack in a single layer. Cook under a preheated broiler for 4–5 minutes on each side or until cooked through. Finish on the skin side so that it is crisp.

Meanwhile, put the noodles in a heatproof bowl, pour over boiling water to cover and stand for 10 minutes, until just tender, then drain. Add the remaining lemon juice, herbs, and cucumber to the noodles and toss well to mix. Season to taste with salt and pepper.

Top the noodles with the cooked chicken and serve immediately, garnished with the chopped red chile.

crispy chicken with salsa verde

Calories per serving **458**
Serves **2**
Preparation time **10 minutes,**
  plus marinating
Cooking time **10 minutes**

2 boneless **chicken breasts,**
  skin on
1 teaspoon **olive oil**
1 **garlic clove,** crushed
1 tablespoon **soy sauce**
new potatoes, to serve

Salsa verde
1 handful **fresh mixed herbs**
  (such as **parsley, thyme,**
  and **basil**)
1 **garlic clove,** coarsely
  chopped
2 **cornichons**
1 tablespoon drained **capers**
1 **anchovy**
2 tablespoons **olive oil**
1 teaspoon **white wine**
  vinegar

Make 3 slashes across the skin side of the chicken breasts and transfer to a nonmetallic dish.

Mix together the oil, garlic, and soy sauce, pour the mixture over the chicken and let marinate for 10 minutes.

Meanwhile, make the salsa verde. Mix all the ingredients together in a blender or food processor until they form a chunky paste. Chill until required.

Heat a ridged grill pan or heavy skillet, add the marinated chicken breasts, skin side down, and fry for 2–3 minutes. Turn and cook for another 3–4 minutes, until they are cooked through.

Serve the chicken with a spoonful of salsa verde and new potatoes (4 per person).

For tomato chicken with Greek salad, prepare the chicken as above, using a marinade of oil, garlic, and 1 tablespoon of tomato paste (omit the soy sauce). Meanwhile, make the Greek salad by tossing together 1 cup halved cherry tomatoes, ¼ chopped cucumber, 1 small diced red onion, and 3 oz crumbled feta cheese. Dress with 1 tablespoon of olive oil and 1 tablespoon red wine vinegar and sprinkle over 1 tablespoon chopped fresh oregano. Season the salad with salt and pepper to taste. Cook the chicken as above and serve with the Greek salad. **Calories per serving 499**

asian steamed chicken salad

Calories per serving **474**
Serves **4**
Preparation time **10 minutes,**
  plus cooling
Cooking time **8–10 minutes**

4 boneless, skinless **chicken
  breasts**, about 5 oz each
½ small **Chinese cabbage,**
  finely shredded
1 large **carrot**, grated
2 cups **bean sprouts**
small bunch of fresh **cilantro,**
  finely chopped
small bunch of **mint**, finely
  chopped
1 **red chile**, seeded and finely
  sliced (optional)

Dressing
½ cup **sunflower oil**
juice of 2 **limes**
1 ½ tablespoons **Thai fish
  sauce**
3 tablespoons **light soy sauce**
1 tablespoon finely chopped
  fresh ginger root

Put the chicken breasts in a bamboo or other steamer
set over a large pan of simmering water. Cover and
let steam for about 8 minutes or until the chicken is
cooked through. Alternatively, poach the chicken for
8–10 minutes, until the meat is cooked and tender.

Meanwhile, make the dressing by mixing together the
ingredients in a bowl.

When the chicken is cool enough to handle, cut or tear
it into strips and mix the pieces with 2 tablespoons of
the dressing. Let cool.

Toss all the vegetables and herbs together and arrange
in serving dishes. Place the cold chicken on top and
serve immediately with the remaining dressing.

For crunchy peanut steamed chicken salad,
finish with 1 tablespoon of crushed unsalted peanuts.
Calories per serving 497

lemon grass chicken

Calories per serving **476**
Serves **4**
Preparation time **15 minutes**
Cooking time **1¾–2¼ hours**

1 tablespoon **sunflower oil**
12 large **chicken drumsticks**
(remove skin before eating)
1 **onion**, finely chopped
4 **garlic cloves**, crushed
6 tablespoons very finely
chopped **lemon grass** and
1 **lemon grass stalk**, halved
lengthwise
1 **red chile**, finely sliced or
chopped
2 tablespoons **medium curry
paste**
1 tablespoon grated **palm
sugar**
1 cup **chicken stock**
salt and **pepper**

Heat the oil in a large, heavy flameproof casserole dish and brown the drumsticks evenly for 5–6 minutes. Remove with a slotted spoon and set aside.

Add the onion and stir-fry over low heat for 10 minutes. Add the garlic, chopped lemon grass, chile, and curry paste and stir-fry for 1–2 minutes.

Return the chicken to the dish with the palm sugar and stock. Bring to a boil, season and cover tightly. Cook in a preheated oven, 275°F, for 1½–2 hours or until tender. Remove from the oven and serve immediately.

For fresh mango salad, as an accompaniment, dice 1 large mango and dress with the zest and juice of 1 lime. Serve cold. **Calories per serving 33**

chicken with burnt chili paste

Calories per serving **479**
Serves **4**
Preparation time **15 minutes**
Cooking time **15 minutes**

2 tablespoons **peanut** or
 vegetable oil
3–4 **dried red chiles**, finely
 chopped
2 **garlic cloves**, thinly sliced
12 oz boneless, skinless
 chicken breasts, cubed
2 tablespoons **Thai fish sauce**
2 tablespoons **water**
2 teaspoons **sugar**
2 **red chiles**, sliced
10 **Thai basil leaves**, plus
 sprigs to garnish
4 **kaffir lime leaves**, shredded
1 cup **roasted cashew nuts**

Burnt chili paste
2 tablespoons **groundnut oil**
1 **red onion**, finely chopped
6–8 large **dried red chiles**,
 finely chopped
6 **garlic cloves**, finely chopped
2 tablespoons **fish sauce**
1 tablespoon **tamarind water**
2 tablespoons packed **brown
 sugar**

Make the burnt chili paste first. Heat the oil in a wok, add the onion, and fry until softened. Remove using a slotted spoon and set aside. Add the chilies and fry until blackened, then remove and set aside. Add the garlic and fry until golden brown, then remove.

Grind half the fried chilies coarsely in a mortar and pestle. Add the onion and garlic and blend to a coarse paste. Return the mixture to the oil remaining in the wok and add the fish sauce, tamarind water, and sugar. Heat gently for 2–3 minutes, stirring constantly, then remove from the heat.

Heat the oil in a wok over high heat until the oil starts to shimmer. Fry the dried chiles until blackened, then remove using a slotted spoon and set aside. Add the sliced garlic to the wok and stir-fry until beginning to brown.

Add the chicken and fry quickly on all sides. Crumble the fried chiles over the chicken and add the burnt chili paste, fish sauce, measured water, sugar, and one of the sliced chiles to the pan. Stir-fry over high heat.

Add the basil leaves, kaffir lime leaves, and cashew nuts and stir-fry for another minute. Garnish with the remaining sliced red chile and the basil sprigs.

For chicken, asparagus, & burnt chili paste, cook the chicken and burnt chili paste as above. Add 7 oz asparagus spears cut in half lengthwise to the pan and stir-fry for 5 minutes before serving. **Calories per serving 491**

sweet-glazed chicken

Calories per serving **482**
(excluding green beans)
Serves **4**
Preparation time **10 minutes**
Cooking time **45 minutes**

2 tablespoons **olive oil**
4 boneless, skinless **chicken
breasts**, about 5 oz each
8 **fresh apricots**, halved and
pitted
2 **pears**, peeled, quartered,
and cored
1 lb **new potatoes**
1 **onion**, cut into wedges
grated zest and juice of
2 **oranges**
a few **thyme sprigs**, chopped
1 tablespoon **whole grain
mustard**
1 tablespoon **honey**
¼ cup **half-fat sour cream**
pepper

To serve
green beans (optional)

Heat the oil in a flameproof casserole, season the
chicken with salt and pepper and add to the pan. Fry
for 2–3 minutes on each side, until golden, then add
the apricots, pears, potatoes, and onion.

Mix together the orange zest and juice, thyme, mustard
and honey and pour over the chicken. Cover the dish
with foil and bake in a preheated oven, 350°F, for 40
minutes, removing the foil halfway through the cooking
time.

When the chicken is cooked, stir the sour cream into
the sauce and serve with green beans, if desired.

chicken & barley

Calories per serving **486**
Serves **4**
Preparation time **15 minutes**
Cooking time **about 1 hour
10 minutes**

2 tablespoons **olive oil**
6 boneless, skinless **chicken
thighs**, diced
1 **onion**, coarsely chopped
2 **garlic cloves**, finely chopped
7 oz **brown mushrooms**,
sliced
1¼ cups **pearl barley**
¾ cup **red wine**
5 cups **chicken stock**
salt and **pepper**
parsley leaves, to garnish

To serve
4 teaspoons **Parmesan
cheese** shavings

Heat the oil in a large skillet over medium-high heat,
add the chicken and onion and fry for 5 minutes, stirring
until lightly browned.

Stir in the garlic and mushrooms and fry for 2 minutes,
then mix in the pearl barley. Add the red wine, half the
stock and season with plenty of salt and pepper, then
bring to a boil, stirring continuously. Reduce the heat,
cover, and simmer for 1 hour, topping up with extra
stock as needed, until the chicken is cooked through
and the barley is soft.

Spoon into shallow bowls and garnish with the parsley.
Sprinkle over the Parmesan shavings and serve.

For chicken & red barley, fry the chicken and
1 chopped red onion as above. Add the garlic and 1 cup
skinned and diced tomatoes, omitting the mushrooms
and pearl barley. Stir in 1¼ cups red Camargue rice, cook
for 1 minute, then add the red wine. Gradually add the hot
stock a small ladleful at a time and stirring constantly, only
adding more once the rice has absorbed the previous
ladleful. Continue until all the liquid has been absorbed
and the chicken and rice are tender. This should take
about 25 minutes. **Calories per serving 452**

chicken tagine

Calories per serving **486**
Serves **4**
Preparation time **20 minutes,**
  plus marinating
Cooking time
  1 hour 40 minutes

8 large boneless, skinless
  chicken thighs or 1 **whole**
  chicken, jointed
1 teaspoon **ground cumin**
1 teaspoon **ground cilantro**
½ teaspoon **ground turmeric**
1 teaspoon **ground ginger**
1 teaspoon **paprika**
3 tablespoons **olive oil**
2 **onions**, cut into wedges
2 **garlic cloves**, finely sliced
1 **fennel bulb**, sliced
10 oz small **new potatoes**
handful of **golden raisins**
8 **ready-to-eat dried apricots**
½ cup **green olives in brine**
  (optional)
pinch of **saffron threads**
1¾ cups hot **chicken stock**
  (see page 14)
small bunch of **fresh cilantro**,
  chopped
salt and **black pepper**

Slash each piece of chicken 2–3 times with a small knife. Mix together the spices and half the olive oil, rub over the chicken pieces, cover, and marinate in the refrigerator for at least 2 hours, preferably overnight.

Heat the remaining oil in a tagine or large flameproof casserole, add the chicken pieces and fry for 4–5 minutes, until golden all over. Add the onion, garlic, and fennel to the pan and continue to fry for 2–3 minutes.

Add all the remaining ingredients, except the cilantro, and stir well. Cover and simmer for about 1½ hours or until the chicken begins to fall off the bone. Season well and stir in the cilantro.

For chicken tagine with prunes & almonds, make the recipe as above, but replace the apricots with 6 chopped prunes. Cover and simmer for about 1½ hours or until the chicken begins to fall off the bone. Stir in 3 tablespoons toasted sliced almonds with the cilantro before serving. **Calories per serving 499**

chicken with black bean sauce

Calories per serving **486**
Serves **4**
Preparation time **10 minutes**
Cooking time **20 minutes**

1 **egg white**
1 tablespoon **cornstarch**
2 boneless, skinless **chicken breasts**, about 13 oz in total, cut into thin strips across the grain
about 1¼ cups **peanut oil**
1 **green bell pepper**, cored, seeded, and cut lengthwise into thin strips
1 **green chile**, deseeded and very finely shredded
4 **garlic cloves**, cut into very thin strips
4 **scallions**, shredded
¼ cup **black bean sauce**
1¼ cups hot **chicken stock**
salt and **pepper**
1–2 heaping tablespoons canned **fermented black beans**, rinsed, to garnish
egg noodles, to serve

Put the egg white into a bowl with a little salt and pepper and whisk with a fork until frothy. Sift in the cornstarch and whisk to mix, then add the chicken and stir until coated.

Heat the oil in a wok until very hot, but not smoking. Add about one-quarter of the chicken strips and stir to separate. Stir-fry for 30–60 seconds, until the chicken turns white on all sides. Lift out with a slotted spoon and drain on paper towels. Repeat with the remaining chicken. Very carefully pour off all but about 1 tablespoon of the hot oil from the wok.

Return the wok to low heat and add the bell pepper, chile, garlic, and about half of the scallions. Stir-fry for a few minutes, until the pepper begins to soften, then add the black bean sauce and stir to mix. Pour in the stock, increase the heat to high and bring to a boil, stirring constantly.

Add the chicken to the sauce and cook over moderate to high heat, stirring frequently, for 5 minutes. Taste for seasoning. Serve hot with egg noodles, garnished with the remaining scallions and the black beans.

grilled chicken with cilantro aïoli

Calories per serving **487**
Serves **4**
Preparation time **15 minutes**
Cooking time **10 minutes**

2 teaspoons coarsely crushed
black peppercorns
4 boneless, skinless **chicken
breasts**, thinly sliced
1 tablespoon **olive oil**

For the cilantro aïoli
small bunch of **fresh cilantro**,
leaves only
1 **garlic clove**, peeled
2 teaspoons **Dijon mustard**
1 **egg yolk**
2 teaspoons **white wine
vinegar**
$^2/_3$ cup **sunflower oil**
salt and **pepper**

To serve
green salad
grated beets

Make the cilantro aïoli. Reserve a few cilantro leaves for garnish and place the rest in a small food processor or blender with the garlic, mustard, egg yolk, and vinegar.

Blend until finely chopped. With the motor running, slowly drizzle in the oil until the mixture is smooth and thick. Season with salt and pepper.

Sprinkle the crushed peppercorns over the chicken slices and drizzle with oil. Cook, in batches, on a preheated hot ridged grill pan for 1–2 minutes on each side or until cooked through and golden.

Garnish the warm chicken slices with the reserved cilantro and serve with the cilantro aïoli, green salad leaves, and grated beets.

For grilled chicken with garlic mayonnaise, thinly slice 4 boneless, skinless chicken breasts, sprinkle with 2 teaspoons coarsely crushed black peppercorns, and drizzle over 1 tablespoon olive oil. Cook, in batches, on a preheated hot ridged grill pan for 1–2 minutes each side or until cooked through and golden. Stir 1 crushed garlic clove into $^2/_3$ cup reduced-fat mayonnaise. Serve with salad greens. **Calories per serving 280**

pan-fried chicken wraps

Calories per serving **487**
Serves **4**
Preparation time **15 minutes**
Cooking time **5 minutes**

1 tablespoon **olive oil**
3 boneless, skinless **chicken
  breasts**, about 5 oz each,
  thinly sliced into strips
3 tablespoons **honey**
1 teaspoon **whole grain
  mustard**
4 **soft flour tortillas**

Coleslaw
¼ small **white cabbage**, finely
  shredded
1 large **carrot**, shredded
3 tablespoons **olive oil**
2 tablespoons **red wine
  vinegar**
1 teaspoon **Dijon mustard**
2 tablespoons chopped
  parsley

Make the coleslaw. Put the white cabbage in a large
mixing bowl with the carrot and toss together well. In a
small bowl whisk together the oil, vinegar, and mustard.
Pour over the cabbage and carrot and toss well to coat.
Add the parsley and toss again. Set aside.

Heat the oil in a large nonstick skillet and cook the
chicken strips over high heat for 4–5 minutes, until
golden and cooked through. Remove from the heat and
add the honey and mustard. Toss well to coat.

Warm the tortillas in a microwave for 10 seconds on
high (or in a warm oven), then spread each with the
coleslaw and top with the chicken pieces. Wrap each
tightly, then cut in half to serve.

For maple-glazed chicken wraps, follow the recipe as
above and toss the cooked chicken with 2 tablespoons
maple syrup (instead of the honey) and the mustard.
Assemble the wraps and serve immediately. **Calories
per serving 499**

chicken skewers with couscous

Calories per serving **496**
Serves **4**
Preparation time **25 minutes,**
  plus marinating
Cooking time **20–25 minutes**

1 lb boneless, skinless
  chicken breasts
2 tablespoons **olive oil**
2 **garlic cloves**, crushed
½ teaspoon each **ground
  cumin, turmeric, paprika**
2 teaspoons **lemon juice**

For the couscous
2 tablespoons **olive oil**
1 small **onion**, finely chopped
1 **garlic clove**, crushed
1 teaspoon each **ground
  cumin, cinnamon, pepper,
  ginger**
⅓ cup **dried dates**
⅓ cup **dried apricots**
¼ cup **blanched almonds**,
  toasted
1 cup **couscous**
2½ cups **vegetable stock**,
  boiling
1 tablespoon **lemon juice**
2 tablespoons chopped **fresh
  cilantro**
salt and **pepper**

Cut the chicken into long thin strips, place them in a
shallow dish and add the olive oil, garlic, spices, and
lemon juice. Stir well, then cover and let marinate
for 2 hours. Thread the chicken strips onto 8 small,
presoaked wooden skewers.

Prepare the couscous by heating half the oil in a
saucepan and frying the onion, garlic, and spices for
5 minutes. Chop and stir in the dried fruits and almonds
and remove from the heat.

Meanwhile, put the couscous in a heatproof bowl, add
the boiling stock, and cover with a dish towel and steam
for 8–10 minutes, until the grains are fluffed up and the
liquid absorbed. Stir in the remaining oil and the fruit
and nut mixture, add the lemon juice and cilantro and
season to taste.

While the couscous is steaming, broil or grill the
chicken skewers for 4–5 minutes on each side, until
charred and cooked through. Serve with the couscous,
garnished with pomegranate seeds, lemon wedges, and
cilantro sprigs, if desired.

For roasted chicken with herb couscous, mix the
oil, garlic, spices, and lemon juice and drizzle over
4 large skinned and slashed chicken thighs. Roast at
375°F for 35–45 minutes. Steam the couscous as
above in stock. Stir in the remaining oil and lemon juice.
Add 4 finely chopped scallions, 3 tablespoons chopped
mint, 3 tablespoons chopped parsley, and 2 chopped
tomatoes. Spoon onto plates, top with the chicken, and
serve with lemon wedges. **Calories per serving 440**

citrus chicken with rice salad

Calories per serving **499**
Serves **2**
Preparation time **10 minutes,**
    plus marinating
Cooking time **15 minutes**

2 boneless, skinless **chicken
    breasts**, sliced lengthwise
    into strips
2 tablespoons **buttermilk**
grated zest and juice of ½
    lime
1 **garlic clove**, crushed

Rice salad
½ cup **mixed basmati** and
    wild rice
1 tablespoon **olive oil**
4 **scallions**, sliced
3 tablespoons **cashew nuts**,
    roughly chopped
handful of **baby leaf spinach**
grated zest and juice of
    1 **orange**
1 tablespoon **soy sauce**

Put the chicken strips in a nonmetallic dish. Mix together the buttermilk, lime zest and juice, and garlic, pour the mixture over the chicken, turn to coat evenly and set aside for at least 10 minutes. Alternatively, prepare the marinade in the morning and leave the chicken in it in the refrigerator all day.

Cook the rice according to the instructions on the package. Drain thoroughly.

Heat the oil in a small skillet. Fry the scallions for 1 minute. Toss the scallions through the rice, and then add the cashew nuts, spinach, orange zest and juice, and soy sauce. Set aside.

Thread the chicken evenly on 4 skewers and cook, turning from time to time, under a preheated hot broiler for 4–5 minutes. Serve with the rice salad.

For coleslaw, as an accompaniment to replace rice salad, finely shred ¼ each of white and red cabbage and 1 carrot. Finely slice ½ red onion and mix everything together in a bowl with 1 tablespoon coarsely chopped parsley. To make the dressing whisk ⅔ cup reduced-fat mayonnaise, ½ tablespoon white wine vinegar, and a pinch of sugar and season with salt and pepper. Toss the dressing through the cabbage mixture and let stand for at least 30 minutes before serving. **Calories per serving 430**

chicken, okra, & red lentil dhal

Calories per serving **499**
Serves **4**
Preparation time **15 minutes**
Cooking time **45 minutes**

2 teaspoons **ground cumin**
1 teaspoon **ground cilantro**
½ teaspoon **cayenne pepper**
¼ teaspoon **ground turmeric**
1 lb boneless, skinless
  chicken thighs, cut into
  large pieces
3 tablespoons **oil**
1 **onion**, sliced
2 **garlic cloves**, crushed
1 tablespoon finely chopped
  fresh ginger root
3 cups **water**
1½ cups **red lentils**, rinsed
7 oz **okra**
small handful of **fresh cilantro**,
  chopped
salt

To serve
lime wedges

Mix together the cumin, cilantro, cayenne, and turmeric and toss with the chicken pieces.

Heat the oil in a large saucepan. Fry the chicken pieces in batches until deep golden, draining each batch to a plate. Add the onion to the pan and fry for 5 minutes, until browned. Stir in the garlic and ginger and cook for another minute.

Return the chicken to the pan and add the measured water. Bring to a boil, then reduce the heat and simmer very gently, covered, for 20 minutes, until the chicken is cooked through. Add the lentils and cook for 5 minutes. Stir in the okra, cilantro and a little salt and cook for another 5 minutes, until the lentils are tender but not completely pulpy.

Check the seasoning and serve in shallow bowls with the lime wedges.

For chicken, zucchini, & chile dhal, use 7 oz zucchini, thinly sliced, instead of the okra. For a hotter flavor, add a thinly sliced medium-strength red chile with the garlic and ginger. **Calories per serving 495**

chicken wrapped in prosciutto

Calories per serving **324**
Serves **4**
Preparation time **10 minutes**
Cooking time **10 minutes**

4 boneless, skinless **chicken
  breasts**, about 5 oz each
4 slices of **prosciutto**
4 **sage leaves**
all-purpose flour, for dusting
2 tablespoons **butter**
2 tablespoons **olive oil**
4 sprigs **cherry tomatoes on
  the vine**
²/₃ cup **dry white wine**
salt and **pepper**
green salad, to serve

Lay each chicken breast between 2 sheets of plastic wrap and flatten with a rolling pin or meat mallet until wafer thin. Season with salt and pepper.

Wrap a slice of prosciutto around each chicken breast, followed by a sage leaf. Secure the sage and prosciutto in position with a toothpick, then lightly dust both sides of the chicken with flour. Season again with salt and pepper.

Heat the butter and oil in a large skillet over high heat, add the chicken, and cook for 4–5 minutes on each side or until the juices run clear when pierced with a knife. Add the tomatoes and wine to the pan and bubble until the wine has thickened and reduced by about half. Serve immediately, with a green salad.

For chicken escalopes with rosemary & pancetta, take 4 chicken breasts, about 4 oz each, and flatten as above. Top each flattened escalope with a sprinkling of rosemary leaves, then wrap each in a slice of pancetta, instead of the prosciutto (omit the sage). Dust with flour, season with salt and pepper, and cook as above.
Calories per serving 335

chicken with red wine & grapes

Calories per serving **368**
Serves **4**
Preparation time **5 minutes**
Cooking time **30 minutes**

3 tablespoons **olive oil**
4 **boneless, skinless chicken breasts**, about 5 oz each
1 **red onion**, sliced
2 tablespoons **red pesto** (see below for homemade)
1 ¼ cups **red wine**
1 ¼ cups **water**
½ cup **red grapes**, halved and seeded
salt and **black pepper**
basil leaves, to garnish

Heat 2 tablespoons of the oil in a large skillet, add the chicken breasts and cook over medium heat for 5 minutes, turning frequently, until browned all over. Remove from the pan with a slotted spoon and drain on paper towels.

Heat the remaining oil in the pan, add the onion slices and pesto and cook, stirring constantly, for 3 minutes, until the onion is softened but not browned.

Add the wine and measured water to the pan and bring to a boil. Return the chicken breasts to the pan and season with salt and pepper to taste. Reduce the heat and simmer for 15 minutes or until the chicken is cooked through.

Stir in the grapes and serve immediately, garnished with basil leaves.

For homemade red pesto, put 1 chopped garlic clove, ½ teaspoon sea salt, ¹/₃ cup basil leaves, 1 cup drained sundried tomatoes in oil, ½ cup extra virgin olive oil, and a little pepper in a food processor or blender and blend until smooth. Transfer to a bowl and stir in 2 tablespoons freshly grated Parmesan cheese.
Calories per serving 368

index

almonds
bell pepper & almond chutney 46
Catalan chicken 202
chicken, apricot, & almond salad 138
chicken tagine with prunes & almonds 218
coronation chicken 58
hot feta & almond quinoa with seared chicken 188
anchovies
chicken Caesar salad 96
warm chicken salad with anchovies 96
apples
barbecued chicken with apple slaw 150
chicken mulligatawny 44
Normandy chicken 202
apricots
chicken & apricot Moroccan couscous 178
chicken, apricot, & almond salad 138
chicken skewers with couscous 226
chicken tagine 218
grilled chicken with apricot & tomato salad 138
sweet-glazed chicken 214
artichokes
celery, artichoke, & chicken salad 198–9
arugula
warm chicken ciabatta with salsa 152
Asian chicken parcels 66
Asian chicken cakes 48
Asian citrus chicken skewers 22
Asian steamed chicken salad 208
asparagus
chicken & asparagus salad 62
chicken, asparagus, & haloumi salad 62
chicken, asparagus, & burnt chili paste 212
chicken with leek & asparagus 94
chicken with spring vegetables 140
green bean & asparagus salad 52
griddled summer chicken salad 132
avocados
chicken, avocado, & coconut salad 176
chicken fajitas & no-chile salsa 194
mango & smoked chicken salad 142

balti chicken 158
bamboo shoots
bamboo chicken with cashews 116
kung po chicken 78
Thai chicken curry 98
barley 216
beans
chicken & adzuki bean salad 176
chicken & asparagus salad 62
chicken with black bean sauce 220
chicken Caesar salad 96
chicken livers with green beans 80
chicken mole 128
chicken teriyaki with beans & cilantro 110
Greek-style chicken 196
green bean & asparagus salad 52
smoked chicken & cannellini bean salad 198
smoked chicken, white bean, & thyme salad 142
Tex-Mex chicken & beans 170
warm chicken salad with anchovies 96
bean sprouts
chicken noodle soup 30
Chinese cabbage & bean sprout salad 48
coconut & chicken soup 30
gingered chicken with bean sprout salad 90
red chicken & coconut broth 106
bell peppers
bell pepper & almond chutney 46
broiled gazpacho chicken salad 134
Caribbean chicken skewers & salsa 60
Caribbean rice salad 60
cashew chicken with peppers 124
cashew chicken with peppers & water chestnuts 124
chicken & adzuki bean salad 176
chicken with black bean sauce 220
chicken ratatouille 108
corn & chicken chowder 86
griddled summer chicken salad 132
quick Chinese-style stir-fry 180
quinoa salad with seared chicken 188
sticky chicken with honey & garlic 24
tandoori chicken skewers 112
wild rice & grilled chicken salad 200
bhoona chicken curry 76
BMI (body mass index) 9
bok choy
Asian chicken parcels 66
chicken & bok choy noodles 122
chicken & shrimp noodles 122
chicken noodle soup 30
chicken with bok choy & shrimp 190
coconut & chicken soup 30
ginger & honey chicken with bok choy 54
miso chicken broth 26
vegetarian nasi goring 68
bread 34, 88, 152, 162
broccoli
chicken fillets with soy glaze 102
chicken with spring vegetables 140
fast chicken curry 182
bulgur wheat 186
Burmese chicken noodle curry 184

calories 8, 10, 12, 13
Caribbean chicken skewers & salsa 60
Caribbean rice salad 60
carrots
chicken & vegetable skewers 24
citrus carrot mulligatawny 44
teriyaki chicken with oriental salad 100
vegetarian nasi goring 68
carving roast chicken 17
cashew nuts
bamboo chicken with cashews 116

cashew chicken with peppers 124
cashew chicken with peppers & water chestnuts 124
citrus chicken with rice salad 228
Catalan chicken 202
celery, artichoke, & chicken salad 198–9
cheese
  chicken & barley 216
  chicken, asparagus, & haloumi salad 62
  chicken tacos 170
  Greek-style chicken 196
  hot feta & almond quinoa with seared chicken 188
  yogurt chicken with Greek salad 186
chiles
  burnt chili paste 212
  chicken & bok choy noodles 122
  chile & cilantro chicken burgers with mango salsa 20
  sweet chili dip 74
  sweet chili sauce 174
Chinese barbecued chicken wings 150
Chinese cabbage
  Chinese cabbage & bean sprout salad 48
  ginger & honey chicken with bok choy 54
  teriyaki chicken with oriental salad 100
chocolate 128
cilantro
  Caribbean chicken skewers & salsa 60
  chile & cilantro chicken burgers with mango salsa 20
  grilled chicken with cilantro aïoli 222

warm lemon chicken & herb salad 56
coconut 60
coleslaw 224, 228
collard greens
  sesame greens with black bean sauce 28
cooked chicken
  chicken mulligatawny 44
  chicken patties with curry sauce 182
  corn & chicken chowder 86
  Greek chicken avgolemono 52
corn
  Caribbean chicken skewers & salsa 60
  chicken & adzuki bean salad 176
  corn & chicken chowder 86
  hot & sour chicken soup 26
  spicy corn chowder 86
  Thai chicken curry 98
  veggie Thai broth 106
coronation chicken 58
couscous
  chicken & apricot Moroccan couscous 178
  chicken couscous salad 144
  chicken with orange & mint 130
  chicken skewers with couscous 226
  grilled chicken & spicy couscous 162
  roasted chicken with herb couscous 226
curries
  balti chicken 158
  bhoona chicken curry 76
  Burmese chicken noodle curry 184
  chicken kofta curry 118
  chicken patties with

curry sauce 182
creamy chicken & vegetable curry 158
curried chicken with mixed vegetables 70
fast chicken curry 182
mild chicken curry with peanuts 116
quick chunky chicken Madras 118
Thai chicken curry 98
tofu noodle curry 184

defrosting 14, 15
deviled chicken 42

eggplants
  chicken ratatouille 108
  curried chicken with mixed vegetables 70
  peppered chicken & eggplant 70
eggs
  chicken Caesar salad 96
  Greek chicken avgolemono 52
  low fat lemon chicken 56
  nasi goring 68
endive 84
exercise 11, 12

fennel
  baked chicken with fennel & potatoes 84
  chicken & fennel stroganoff 146
  chicken tikka sticks & fennel 46
  fennel, lemon, & honey smoked chicken 120
frozen chicken 14, 15

garlic
  grilled chicken with garlic mayonnaise 222
  sticky chicken with honey & garlic 24
  tangy chicken, lemon, &

garlic toasties 88
gazpacho soup with chicken salsa 134
ginger
  Asian chicken cakes 48
  Asian chicken parcels 66
  Caribbean chicken skewers & salsa 60
  chicken & bok choy noodles 122
  chicken & shrimp noodles 122
  chicken breasts with oriental glaze 102
  chicken with leek & asparagus 94
  chicken livers with green beans 80
  chicken tikka sticks & fennel 46
  crispy spiced chicken wings 74
  ginger & honey chicken 54
  gingered chicken with bean sprout salad 90
  gingered chicken with soft noodles 90
  miso chicken broth 26
  rice with leeks, ginger, & cumin 94
  Szechuan chicken 28
  Thai sesame chicken patties 126
grapes
  chicken with red wine & grapes 234
Greek chicken avgolemono 52
Greek salad with mixed herb dressing 196
Greek-style chicken 196
ground chicken
  Asian chicken cakes 48
  balti chicken 158
  chicken burgers & tomato salsa 20

chicken kofta curry 118
chicken mole 128
chicken tacos 170
chile & cilantro chicken
burgers with mango
salsa 20
mini chicken meatballs
with pimento purée
154
Tex-Mex chicken &
beans 170
Thai sesame chicken
patties 126

harissa
grilled harissa chicken
168
Moroccan chicken &
harissa 192
healthy eating 12–13
honey
fennel, lemon, & honey
smoked chicken 120
ginger & honey chicken
54
sticky chicken with
honey & garlic 24
hygiene essentials 14

jerk chicken 42
jerk chicken wings 156
jointing 16

kung po chicken 78

leeks
chicken with leek &
asparagus 94
one-pot chicken 84
rice with leeks, ginger, &
cumin 94
lemon grass chicken 210
lemons
Asian citrus chicken
skewers 22
chicken with rosemary
& lemon 130
citrus carrot
mulligatawny 44

fennel, lemon, & honey
smoked chicken 120
Greek chicken
avgolomeno 52
herby quinoa with lemon
178
lemony poached
chicken 160
low-fat lemon chicken
56
piri piri chicken skewers
22
tangy chicken, lemon, &
garlic toasties 88
warm lemon chicken &
herb salad 56
lentils
chicken mulligatawny
44
chicken, okra, & red
lentil dhal 230
citrus carrot
mulligatawny 44
lettuce
chicken Caesar salad
96
gingered chicken with
bean sprout salad 90
spiced chicken &
mango salad 58
teriyaki chicken with
three seeds 100
limes
bhoona chicken curry
76
spiced roast chicken
with lime 136
tandoori chicken
skewers 112
teriyaki chicken with
three seeds 100
liver
chicken livers with
green beans 80
ginger & honey chicken
54
warm chicken liver salad
80
low-fat products 8

mangoes
chile & cilantro chicken
burgers with mango
salsa 20
fresh mango salad 210
mango & smoked
chicken salad 142
spiced chicken &
mango salad 58
maple-glazed chicken
wraps 224
Mediterranean chicken
parcels 66
Mediterranean pasta
salad 172
mint
chicken with orange &
mint 130
miso chicken broth 26
miso broiled chicken 72
Moroccan chicken &
harissa 192
mushrooms
chicken & barley 216
chicken ratatouille 108
hot & sour chicken soup
26
vegetarian nasi goring
68
mustard
smoked mustard
chicken 120

nasi goring 68
noodles
Burmese chicken
noodle curry 184
chicken & bok choy
noodles 122
chicken & shrimp
noodles 122
Chicken noodle soup
30
chicken teriyaki 110
gingered chicken with
soft noodles 90
noodles & seven-spice
chicken 190
rice noodles with lemon

chicken 204
Thai chicken noodle
salad 172
tofu noodle curry 184
Normandy chicken 202

obesity 9
okra
chicken, okra, & red
lentil dhal 230
olives
Greek-style chicken
196
Mediterranean chicken
parcels 66
one-pot chicken 84
oranges
chicken with orange &
mint 130
chicken, tarragon, &
orange salad 64
chicken, tarragon, &
orange tagliatelle 64
citrus carrot
mulligatawny 44
citrus chicken with rice
salad 228
jerk chicken 42
wild rice, orange, &
haloumi salad 200

pancakes 82
pancetta
chicken escalopes with
rosemary & pancetta
232
pasta
chicken minestrone 32
chicken, tarragon, &
orange tagliatelle 64
Greek chicken
avgolomeno 52
Mediterranean pasta
salad 172
peanut butter
chicken satay 72
satay chicken pancakes
82
Thai chicken satay 166

peanuts
  Chinese cabbage &
  bean sprout salad 48
  crunchy peanut
  steamed chicken salad
  208
  gingered chicken with
  soft noodles 90
  kung po chicken 78
  mild chicken curry with
  peanuts 116
pears 214
peppered chicken &
  eggplant 70
peppered chicken
  skewers 50
pesto 234
physical activity 11
pineapple
  Caribbean chicken
  skewers & salsa 60
  pineapple salsa 114
pine nuts
  chicken, raisin, & pine
  nut pilau 104
  warm chicken & pine
  nut salad 104
piri piri chicken skewers 22
pomegranates
  chicken couscous salad
  144
  pomegranate raita 112
potatoes
  baked chicken with
  fennel & potatoes 84
  chicken tagine 218
  corn & chicken chowder
  86
  griddled summer
  chicken salad 132
  one-pot chicken 84
  spiced roast chicken
  with lime 136
  spicy corn chowder 86
  sweet-glazed chicken
  214
poussins 16–17
preparing chicken 15
prosciutto 232

prunes
  chicken tagine with
  prunes & almonds 218

quinoa
  herby quinoa with lemon
  178
  hot feta & almond
  quinoa with seared
  chicken 188
  quinoa salad with
  seared chicken 188

raisins
  Catalan chicken 202
  chicken, raisin, & pine
  nut pilau 104
  warm chicken & pine
  nut salad 104
raita, pomegranate 112
red barley
  chicken & red barley
  216
red chicken & coconut
  broth 106
refreezing chicken 14
reheating food 14
rice
  Caribbean rice salad 60
  chicken & spinach curry
  40
  chicken, raisin, & pine
  nut pilau 104
  citrus chicken with rice
  salad 228
  coconut rice 78
  miso chicken broth 26
  nasi goring 68
  rice with leeks, ginger, &
  cumin 94
  Thai chicken shells with
  cilantro 180
  vegetable chicken &
  rice 32
roast chicken
  carving 17
rosemary
  chicken escalopes
  with rosemary &

pancetta 232
  chicken with rosemary
  & lemon 130

salsa
  Caribbean salsa 60
  chicken fajitas & no-
  chile salsa 194
  chicken salsa 134
  mango salsa 20
  pineapple salsa 114
  tomato salsa 114, 152
salsa verde 120, 206
satay
  Asian chicken cakes
  48
  chicken satay 72
  satay chicken pancakes
  82
  Thai chicken satay 166
sesame seeds
  chicken & bok choy
  noodles 122
  chicken & sweet chili
  sesame skewers 50
  sesame greens with
  black bean sauce 28
  teriyaki chicken with
  three seeds 100
  Thai sesame chicken
  patties 126
sherried chicken
  stroganoff 146
shrimp
  chicken & shrimp
  noodles 122
  chicken with bok choy &
  shrimp 190
  nasi goring 68
skewers
  Asian citrus chicken 22
  Caribbean chicken &
  salsa 60
  chicken & sweet chili
  sesame 50
  chicken & vegetable 24
  chicken skewers with
  couscous 226
  masala chicken

kebabs 76
  peppered chicken
  skewers 50
  piri piri chicken skewers
  22
  tandoori chicken
  skewers 38, 112
smoked chicken
  chicken & asparagus
  salad 62
  fennel, lemon, & honey
  smoked chicken 120
  mango & smoked
  chicken salad 142
  smoked chicken
  bruschetta 34
  smoked chicken toasts
  34
  smoked mustard
  chicken 120
spatchcocking 16–17
spinach
  chicken & spinach curry
  40
  citrus chicken with rice
  salad 228
  spinach salad 102
  vegetable chicken &
  rice 32
stock, chicken 15
sweet potato mash 156
Szechuan chicken 28

tacos 170, 194
tandoori chicken
  grilled tandoori chicken
  168
  tandoori chicken
  salad 38
  tandoori chicken
  skewers 38, 112
teriyaki chicken
  chicken teriyaki 110
  chicken teriyaki with
  beans & cilantro 110
  teriyaki chicken with
  oriental salad 100
  teriyaki chicken with
  three seeds 100

Tex-Mex chicken & beans 170

Thai chicken
homemade green Thai curry paste 98
hot & sour chicken soup 26
red chicken & coconut broth 106
Thai barbecued chicken 174
Thai chicken curry 98
Thai chicken noodle salad 172
Thai chicken satay 166
Thai chicken shells with cilantro 180
Thai sesame chicken patties 126

tofu noodle curry 184

tomatoes
broiled gazpacho chicken salad 134
chicken & asparagus salad 62
chicken & spinach curry 40
chicken burgers & tomato salsa 20
chicken mole 128
chicken mulligatawny 44
chicken ratatouille 108
chicken wrapped in prosciutto 232
fast chicken curry 182
Greek-style chicken 196
griddled salsa chicken 114
grilled chicken with apricot & tomato salad 138
hot tomato, caramelized onion & chicken open sandwich 152
Mediterranean chicken parcels 66
smoked chicken bruschetta 34
smoked chicken toasts 34
sticky chicken with honey & garlic 24
tomato chicken with Greek salad 206
warm chicken salad with anchovies 96
wild rice & grilled chicken salad 200
yogurt chicken with Greek salad 186

tortillas 132, 194, 224

vegetables
Asian citrus chicken skewers 22
baby leaf stir-fry with chili 126
chicken & vegetable skewers 24
chicken minestrone 32
chicken with spring vegetables 140
creamy chicken & vegetable curry 158
curried chicken with mixed vegetables 70
gingered chicken with soft noodles 90
vegetable chicken & rice 32

vegetarian nasi goring 68
veggie Thai broth 106

water chestnuts
cashew chicken with peppers & water chestnuts 124

whole chicken
carving 17
checking if cooked 15
jointing 16

wild rice
wild rice & grilled chicken salad 200
wild rice, orange, & haloumi salad 200

wine
chicken with red wine & grapes 234

yogurt
bhoona chicken curry 76
chicken & spinach curry 40
chicken kofta curry 118
chicken tacos 170
chicken tikka sticks & fennel 46
coronation chicken 58
pomegranate raita 112
seared chicken sandwich 88
spiced chicken & mango salad 58
tandoori chicken salad 38
tandoori chicken skewers 38, 112
yogurt chicken & bulgur wheat salad 186
yogurt chicken with Greek salad 186

acknowledgments

Commissioning editor: Eleanor Maxfield
Designer: Jeremy Tilston
Editor: Pauline Bache
Production controller: Sarah Kramer

Octopus Publishing Group 65, 73; David Loftus 9, 175, 213; David Munns 1, 11, 14, 15, 16, 17, 23, 27, 61, 71, 89, 91, 97, 101, 127, 129, 147, 151, 155, 165, 189, 203, 217; Gareth Sambidge 235; Ian Wallace 18, 36, 67, 99, 166, 221, 227; Lis Parsons 2, 25, 33, 35, 41, 103, 105, 135, 137, 139, 145, 153, 171, 179, 181, 187, 191, 195, 197, 199, 215, 223, 225, 231; Peter Myers 55; Sean Myers 4, 29, 43, 49, 133, 169, 193; Stephen Conroy 6, 8, 51, 83, 92, 109, 115, 131, 141, 157, 173, 183, 185, 205, 207, 209, 211, 229, 233; Will Heap 12, 31, 69, 75, 77, 81, 95, 111, 113, 119, 121, 123, 125, 149, 159; William Lingwood 59, 63, 143; William Reavell 57, 79, 87, 117; William Shaw 10, 13, 21, 39, 45, 47, 53, 85, 107, 161, 163, 177, 201, 219.